FROM CHANNEL ROW TO CABRA

This book is dedicated to my parents
May and William P. Kealy
in loving memory and gratitude

From Channel Row to Cabra

DOMINICAN NUNS AND THEIR TIMES 1717-1820

Máire M. Kealy OP

the columba press

First published in 2010 by
the columba press
55A Spruce Avenue, Stillorgan Industrial Park,
Blackrock, Co Dublin

Cover by Bill Bolger
Origination by The Columba Press
Printed in Ireland by ColourBooks Ltd, Dublin

ISBN 978 1 85607 693-7

Contents

In Memory of
Mother Mary of Jesus Bellew
Mother Elizabeth of the Holy Ghost Weever
Mother Julia of Jesus Browne
Sister Mary Rice
Sister Mary of the Holy Ghost Vaughan
and
Helena Keating, Sister Mary of the Rosary of St Dominic
who
in evil days and after many tribulations founded
in North Brunswick Street
the first Convent of the Order
in Dublin AD 1717.
100 years later the Community then consisting of five Sisters
removed to St Mary's Cabra.

Foreword

by Margaret Mac Curtain

Eighteenth-century Ireland swings open and shut like a door on hinges. It closes on an Ireland which had allied itself with the restored Stuart monarchy in 1660 and fought unsuccessfully its last stand for King James II at the battle of Aughrim; and it opens on a scene where the Irish supporters of King William of Orange seized power and imposed a stringent set of penal laws on both Catholic and Protestant dissenter. Dr Kealy's study of Dominican nuns from 1717 to 1820 begins with the change over to the Hanoverian monarchy, a very slight mitigation of the worst of the penal laws and the retreat of the Irish Catholic gentry that they were losers in the stakes, with shrinking fortunes and family lands. The country settled down to a long period of outward conformity to the ruling class, the self-styled Ascendancy.

Dr Kealy's women are drawn from the Anglo-Irish gentry who did not belong to the Ascendancy; they were the descendants of the sixteenth-century recusant Catholics who were categorised a century later as 'papists' in the terminology of the penal laws. Catholicism was integral to their identity. Her study gives the reader an intimate and rare picture of how women from this land-owning elite survived in the teeth of seemingly insurmountable obstacles. Máire Kealy infects new meaning into a familiar script of how life was for Catholics in eighteenth-century Ireland. Her women elected to become Dominican nuns, described in an eighteenth-century state document as 'Mrs Bellew's family in Channel Row' and they lived in a large but unobtrusive dwelling in Channel Row in Oxmantown just outside the city of Dublin boundaries under the very eyes of the law across the river from Dublin Castle. The four-storey building provided space for a small community of Dominican nuns, their chapel, rooms for retired ladies and a boarding school for the education of children. Incredibly, they escaped eviction and possible exile at a time when periodic raids on houses reported to be convents, nunneries or monasteries were frequent.

Originally the Channel Row group was part of the Galway monastery whose history Sister Rose O'Neill wrote, *A Rich Inheritance, Galway Dominican Nuns 1644-1994*, and they came to Dublin for a more secure foundation such was the uncertainty of maintaining a monastery in Galway. Why Dublin, into the jaws of the law-enforcers? Eighteenth-century Dublin was a kind of melting-pot about to be transformed into Georgian Dublin, where cultural, political and religious strands mingled in all sorts of intriguing patterns. It was daunting but manageable to remain invisible in Dublin provided one had the right connections. Mary Bellew and the group of five nuns she led were related to the leading Old English and Anglo-Irish gentry, landed country families who had friends and relatives in government but who themselves chose to be Catholic and in many cases Jacobites.

We learn about the background of the Channel Row inhabitants from this captivating narrative. Mary Bellew was one of the Bellews of Barmeath, Co Louth, the senior branch of a family who suffered transplantation into Connacht in the previous century but who managed to hold on to their property in Barmeath to the present day. Mary and Catherine Plunkett were closely related to Saint Oliver Plunkett; Ellen Keating's father was a prominent Jacobite and supporter of King James II. Eliza Weever's origins have proved elusive, possibly Co Clare, and Julia Browne's story is a cameo of the spectre of banishment that was always in the background of the group. The founding group was joined by others whose names reveal the close-knit connections within the Catholic network of eighteenth-century Ireland: the O'Reillys of Lower Breffney, the Rices, The Taaffes, the Kellys, and the Vaughans; by mid-century the community of nuns numbered twenty-seven. Equally revealing were the names of the two daughters of Lord Mayo, two Nugents, daughters of Lord Riverston of Westmeath, one Browne, a daughter of Lord Kenmare, two Plunketts, daughters of Lord Dunsany, two Barnwalls, daughters of Lord Trimleston, a daughter of Lady Cavan, and two daughters of Viscount Netterville. Yet another dimension to the activities of Channel Row is supplied by the ladies who retired to live within the precincts of the convent.

According to Mrs Delany, the diarist, the best gossip was to be found in the parlours of Channel Row Convent.

Dr Kealy has drawn on the account books of Channel Row, the early annals and other documents in the Cabra archives as well as the history of Dublin banking, the newspapers of the period, the growing list of published research on eighteenth-century Ireland, but she has put her own stamp on the story she . writes here. By examining a group such as the Dominican nuns of Channel Row she has introduced a new methodology which gives the reader access to a hidden lifestyle, the finances behind that way of living, the personalities of those who lived in the large house. Their shared culture becomes visible, their family networks; they belonged to an elite and the reader observes with sadness their decline towards the end of the century. The surprise factor of course is their ability to survive and Máire Kealy leaves another five founding women to begin a new and successful chapter in Cabra on 12 December 1819. Eliza Byrne formed the link between Channel Row and the new foundation in Cabra and the new century brought a generation of women with entrepreneurial skills into focus. In the decades following the amalgamation of autonomous Dominican convents (1928) Mary Bellew and her family in Channel Row gained a folklorish stature which was enhanced by the storytelling skills of great prioresses–general, Mother Colmcille Flynn and Mother Reginald Lyons. What Máire Kealy has accomplished is making real those folkloric figures, convincing the relationships with other elements of Dublin society, their contribution to liturgy in the city and above all their freedom to negotiate living in unsettled times.

Margaret Mac Curtain

Introduction

Not many people walking or driving up and down North Brunswick Street in Dublin today are aware that until late in the eighteenth century this street was called Channel Row and that a community of Dominican nuns lived in a large house sited on the north side of the street. In those days, all women religious were officially called 'Nuns', as distinct from 'Sisters'. In the early twentieth century a new code of canon law distinguished between two categories of religious women: nuns and religious sisters. Officially, the term 'nuns' describes women who take solemn religious vows, are strictly enclosed from 'the world' and whose lifestyle is centred on contemplative prayer and the recitation of the divine office of the church. Religious women who engaged in any of the ministries of teaching, nursing, and/or tending to the needs of the poor and other apostolic work are today known as 'religious sisters'. Religious sisters take simple vows and are free to travel outside their convents, visit the sick in their own homes, teach in schools, nurse in hospitals and do other kinds of work according to the needs of the people at any given time. According to canon law, for religious the distinction between solemn and simple vows refers mainly to strict enclosure and matters of property and inheritance. The present-day Irish (Cabra) Dominicans, whose origins date back to the Galway Dominican community and to Channel Row, are more properly called 'religious sisters'. However, in our narrative, to avoid confusion and to keep the story in its historical context and in line with the way of speech of that era, the term 'nuns' is generally used for the Dominicans of Channel Row and other religious sisters referred to in the story.

In Ireland the eighteenth and nineteenth centuries saw the emergence of a number of individuals and groups of women who have had enormous influence on Irish education, health care, and social welfare. This is particularly true of the newly founded religious congregations. Towards the end of the eighteenth century these Irish congregations were spearheaded by Nano Nagle (1718-84) who founded the Presentation Sisters in Cork. Nano's interest was in the education of the poor and she was followed in the nineteenth century by four other women: Catherine McAuley (1781-1841) who founded the Sisters of Mercy, Mary Aikenhead (1787-1858) who founded the Irish Sisters of Charity (now known as the Religious Sisters of Charity) and Margaret Aylward (1810-89) who founded the Sisters of the Holy Faith. Margaret's interest was in children who were orphaned or in need of care and for whom no adequate provision was made to have them brought up in the Catholic faith. Frances Ball, in 1821, at the invitation of the Archbishop of Dublin, Dr Murray (1768-1852), introduced to Ireland the Institute of the Blessed Virgin Mary of the Bar Convent in York England, and these nuns became popularly known in Ireland as the Loreto Sisters. These Irish-founded congregations catered for the educational and health needs of the people and the emphasis in many cases was on ministry to the poor.

The Dominican community of Channel Row, who came from Galway in 1717, was the only group of nuns in Dublin which succeeded in keeping a boarding school open throughout the period of the Penal Laws. In eighteenth-century Dublin, Carmelite and Augustinian nuns each set up a boarding school south of the Liffey for the daughters of the Catholic nobility and gentry, but neither of these schools survived. The history of the Channel Row nuns has never been fully documented or published. Sr Genevieve Mooney OP pioneered research into the story of the convent when in 1968 she presented an excellent paper, 'Mrs Bellew's Family', to the Dublin Historical Society.[1] This paper sparked off my interest in delving further into that period of our history and this present volume is the result.

The original work was in the form of a dissertation presented

---

1. G. Mooney, 'Mrs Bellew's Family', *Dublin Historical Record*, Vol XXII (Oct 1968)

for an MA degree in Lancaster University. I am indebted to Dr
Sarah Barber, my supervisor and Senior Lecturer in the history
department in the university, for her help at that time. Mr Seán
O Boyle of The Columba Press Dublin kindly accepted the manuscript for publication and has given me every help in publish-
ing it. I am grateful to all librarians in Dublin City Libraries,
particularly the Pearse Street, City Archives branch and to the
staffs of the National Library and National Archives, Dublin for
their unfailing courtesy at all times.

I owe an immense debt of gratitude to my Dominican Sisters
at generalate, regional and community levels and to our two
archivists, Srs Mary O'Byrne and Maris Stella McKeown for
their support and encouragement in having this book produced.
Sr Rose O'Neill as always, was generous with her time and in
giving me access to archival material from the Galway convent
archives in Taylor's Hill. Dr Margaret MacCurtain graciously
agreed to write the Foreword and I am grateful to her for her unfailing help at all times. I wish to thank Mr Dominic McNamara,
Assistant to the President of St Patrick's College Maynooth, for
permission to use material from the catalogue, Maynooth
College Bicentenary Art Exhibitions (Maynooth: 1995). My
grateful thanks are due also to my nephew John Kealy who once
again helped me with photographs.

One of the most rewarding aspects of the research was to
meet personally or by correspondence, some of the families
directly connected with the Dominican Convent, Channel Row.
We Dominican women of the twenty-first century owe so much
to the courage and determination of all these eighteenth-century
nuns who persevered in spite of their difficulties and handed on
the inheritance to us. The Honourable Bryan Bellew and his wife
Rosemary, of Barmeath Castle, Co Louth, are direct relatives of
Mary Bellew and Sir John Nugent and his wife Lady Penelope,
of Ballinlough Castle, Co Westmeath, are direct relatives of the
Reillys and Nugents. The Bellew, Browne and (O') Reilly / Nugent
families have been very helpful to me in researching material for
this book. Sadly Sir John Nugent died in November 2009, may
he rest in peace; his Reilly / Nugent family roots date back to the
Milesian sept of O'Reilly of Lower Breffny.

Two other connections with the Channel Row convent were

in contact by post, as the families now reside in England. One of these is the Earl of Westmeath, a member of another branch of the Nugent family. The present earl was unable to help with any family documentation as the papers had been burned but he gave some information about the title Riverston. The head of this branch of the Nugent family, Thomas Nugent, was given the title of Marquisite of Riverston by King James II in 1689 but the title was never recognised by the English House of Lords. In recent times, Dublin Corporation named a new estate near the Navan Road in Dublin, 'Riverston Abbey' in recognition of this indirect link with Dominican Convent, Cabra. The Browne family also corresponded by post. The document supplied by John Kilmaine was proof that Julia Browne of Channel Row was a daughter of the Browne family of the Neale, Co Mayo. Julia's story is full of surprises. The family title Barons of Kilmaine was bestowed presumably on Julia's father, John Browne in 1726 and he was known as Sir John Browne. Finding these living links with the families was an emotional experience and helped to bring to life these eighteenth-century ladies, Mary Bellew, the Reilly sisters, Catherine and Mary, the Nugents and of course. Julia Browne.

CHAPTER ONE

Early History[2]

The early history of the Cabra Dominicans (Ireland) which orig-
inated in Galway in 1647 and in Channel Row Dublin in 1717 is
inextricably woven into Irish political and church history. The
upheavals and instability of society during the seventeenth and
eighteenth centuries had an impact on the lives of all the people
in the country and Dominican nuns were no exception in those
turbulent times. Political events influenced the lives of these
women and so the narrative will move back and forth between
the political scene and the cloister. The earliest recorded and
documented date of our Galway nuns is associated with the
Confederation of Kilkenny in 1644. This followed the recognition and approval of the nuns' convent by the provincial chapter
of the Dominican friars in 1643. The Confederation of Kilkenny
was a provisional parliament chosen from among those who
represented the Catholic population; it was set up in Kilkenny in
the immediate wake of the Rising of 1641 and at the end of the
1644 war. Its members were called 'the Confederate Catholics of
Ireland'.[3] The Pope sent an envoy to the Confederates, Giovanni
Battista Rinuccini; Rinuccini visited the Galway convent in 1647
and gave the nuns a document which 'confirmed by letters
patent of the Holy See the new foundation, conferring on it the
status of a monastery with papal protection and all the privileges enjoyed by such an establishment'.[4] This was the approval
the Dominican nuns sought.

---

2. It should be noted that English standardised spelling was not introduced until after 1755 when Samuel Johnson published *A Dictionary of
the English Language*. All quotations therefore, from the Account Books
of Channel Row use the original eighteenth-century spelling without
alteration to modern spelling.
3. J. C. Beckett, *The Making of Modern Ireland, 1603-1923* (London: 1966)
p 89
4. R. O'Neill, *A Rich Inheritance* (Galway: 1994) p 10

The Dominican women are not as fortunate as the Dominican friars in preserving their written records. There is incidental evidence of the presence of Dominican women in Ireland prior to 1644. Some examples will suffice to establish the reality of their presence whether they were 'nuns', i.e. living in community, or perhaps lay women either married or single, who had joined the third order of Saint Dominic and continued to live in their own homes. These pieces of evidence generally relate to the west of Ireland but in particular to counties Galway, Mayo, and Roscommon. The evidence is fragmentary and scattered but is there nevertheless. The first book published in Louvain in 1706, which mentions the nuns is O'Heyne's *The Irish Dominicans*. O'Heyne writes: '... I do not know how many years back, [the nuns were in Galway] although I think it was at the end of the reign of James I'.[5] This would place the foundation sometime in or around 1625. In the Taylor's Hill convent archives there are some transcripts from a book published in 1840, *Educational History of Ireland*. The author, a Father Delaney, refers to an eye-witness' statement that '... [there were] very few monasteries of nuns of any of the mendicant orders [Franciscan, Dominican and Carmelites] before the fall of Henry VIII,' and goes on to say that from the registry of the Master General there is evidence of some [Dominicans] 'in the south in the time of Henry VIII'.[6] Another reference from that source states: 'on 8 March 1549, Fr N. is appointed commissary of all convents, monasteries *of both sexes* of the Province of Ireland with full authority.'[7]

The Effect of the Penal Laws on Dominican Women in Ireland
The Penal Laws were first enacted in the time of Elizabeth I in 1558. New statutes were frequently added and continued to multiply over a period of two hundred years. Ultimately Catholic Emancipation in 1829 gave complete freedom of religion to the Catholics and various later reforms relating to the

5. J. O'Heyne, *The Irish Dominicans of the Seventeenth Century* (Louvain: 1706) p 157
6. Rev M. J. Brennan OSF, 1840. No publisher given
7. B/33, Book 4, Archives, Taylor's Hill convent, notes in manuscript copybook. Italics added

franchise, gave Catholics the right to vote in political elections. The motivation for the Penal Laws was to 'prevent the further growth of popery' and deprive the Catholic population in particular from having any power, civil or religious, and if possible to convert Catholics to the Protestant religion.[8] The laws were particularly harsh in the sphere of freedom of religion and land-ownership and were intended to disinherit Catholics and deprive them of the right to pass on their holdings to their heirs unless the heirs committed themselves to the Protestant faith. The Penal Laws had a profound effect and extended to education and the professions. Catholics were not alone in suffering from this penal code; it affected others – Protestant dissenters in particular.

Given this background of penal measures and the active persecution of Catholics, and in particular of priests and religious, it is not surprising that the Dominican women may have been cautious of keeping records which might incriminate themselves or their relatives. The women Dominicans were not as numerous as the friars and were scattered; sometimes they were in hiding among their own relatives or in small groups of two or three together in remote areas of the countryside. Persecution of those who refused to conform to the Penal Laws was at times very severe and at other times the pressures were relaxed, according to the prevailing political climate. Indeed the political climate was the key factor in the timing of the pursuit of priests, religious of both sexes, and of anyone suspected of having schools or 'subverting the state'. After the Reformation the dissolution of the monasteries was a major upheaval for Catholics. The period of Elizabeth's reign (1558-1603) was a dark one when priests both secular and religious were hunted, exiled, and if found in Ireland, very often executed. Later in the seventeenth century, in the Cromwellian era, whenever there was rumour or a threat of a Stuart restoration to the throne of England, life was made very difficult for everyone suspected of or presumed to be in favour of the Stuarts repossessing the throne.

---

8. For Example, various Acts such as: 7 Will III, c.4 (1695) To restrain foreign education; 2 Anne c.6 (1703) to restrain the growth of popery and others relating to religion; 1 George II c.20 (1727) Act to regulate the Admission of Barristers at Law

Traces of Dominican Women: The Two Honorias

During the Cromwellian period 1649-58 there were particularly vicious attempts to track down and either exile or kill anyone, lay or religious, who might be involved. Two Dominican women, Honoria Burke, (also called de Burgo) and Honoria Magaen, both living in Co Mayo, met their deaths in this period. Honoria Burke lived near Burrishoole and was received into the Order by the provincial Thaddeus Mac Duane, sometime around 1583-85. Thaddeus was a Dominican of wide experience of life in sixteenth-century Rome and Ireland.[9] In 1653 it is held that the soldiers were in pursuit of Fr Felix O'Conor, prior of Burrishoole, who with some other friars escaped to Clare Island. Honoria Burke ran into the woods nearby to escape capture but she was caught by the soldiers and severely beaten; she later died from her injuries. In the Acts of the General Chapter of the Order 1656 she is expressly named as a martyr. In the same era Honoria Magaen, also in flight from the soldiers, climbed into a hollowed-out tree to hide; she died of exposure to the cold and her body was later found in the tree.[10] These two women, Burke and Magaen, are proof that not all Dominican nuns were able to live safely in community. Devotion to Honoria Magaen as a martyr spread as far as Taormina in Sicily where a fresco in a church in the town depicts her frozen body in a tree.

There were Third Order women living 'in and around the town' of Ballinrobe, Co Mayo, until the late nineteenth century. These women lived singly in their own houses and were noted for their piety and simple lifestyle; they were the remnants of a thriving group from earlier years and most likely kept to the traditions of their predecessors. Their habit was

> a long black robe with a thick leather belt and a large crucifix attached. Over this they wore a long black cloak with a hood. Their head-dress was a black bonnet fringed with white rucking[11]

9. T. S. Flynn, *The Irish Dominicans 1536-1641* (Dublin: Four Courts Press, 1993) pp 79, 87

10. Daphne D. C. Pochin Mould, *The Irish Dominicans*, (Dublin: Dominican Publications, 1957) p 130

11. B. Mulloy, *Itchy Feet and Thirsty Work, a Guide to the History and Folklore of Ballinrobe* (Mayo: Lough Mask and Lough Garra Tourist Development Association. nd)

These Ballinrobe Dominicans wore their habits only when going to Mass and when visiting the old and the sick; at other times they wore the ordinary clothes of the time. They celebrated the feast of St Dominic on 4 August annually with special devotion and prayed in their own homes at eleven o'clock each day. The home of a Dominican could be recognised by the special crest over the door and they had their own special burial plot at Teampall na Leaca near Ballinrobe. Information about them is vague due to lack of documentation but again it is thought that they had their small convents during the penal days and continued in some manner until 1880.[12] As a direct consequence of the Penal Laws in Ireland, a Dominican convent was founded in 1639 in Lisbon, Portugal, called Convento do Bom Sucesso, to cater for young Irish women who wished to join the Order.[13] This is another proof that life as a nun in Ireland was almost impossible. Other traces of Dominican women whether nuns or third order members are found in passing comments in the history of the friars. In one instance, directions were given that a chalice dated 1634 and which belonged to Father Terence Coghlan, was to be given to his relation, Eleanor Callanan, 'a religious of the Dominican family'.[14] These are some of the signposts to Dominican women who undoubtedly existed in the sixteenth and seventeen centuries before the Chapter of 1643 and the visit of the nuncio Cardinal Rinucini to Galway in 1644. The Chapter and the nuncio gave the Galway Dominican nuns the approval of both the Dominican Order and the pope. In the next chapter the history of the Galway Dominican convent will be summarised. This convent was sited in the centre of Galway City in the seventeenth and eighteenth centuries. It is now sited on Taylor's Hill, and is the first documented foundation of Dominican nuns in Ireland.

There was one eighteenth-century foundation of Dominican nuns which made a brave but unsuccessful effort to establish itself in Waterford. In 1725 the general chapter of the friars held in

---

12. B. Mulloy, *Itchy Feet and Thirsty Work*
13. For the history of the Lisbon convent, see Honor McCabe OP, *A Light Undimmed* (Dublin: Dominican Publications, 2007)
14. L. Taheny OP, *The Dominicans of Roscommon* (Dublin: St Mary's Priory, Tallaght) p 16

Bologna ordered that a convent of nuns should be restored in the city of Waterford. It was to replace a convent of pre-Reformation times, which 'will be an ornament to the Catholic religion, [and a] means to instruct the young ladies of this city and country in piety and Christian education'.[15] By the command of Father Thomas Ripoll, Master of the order, two nuns were sent to Waterford by the Irish provincial prior, Father Bernard MacHenry. One was Sr Anastasia Wyse a member of a prominent family in Waterford who was at the time a member of the Channel Row community in Dublin. The second person was Sr Margaret Brown of the Galway community; both of these nuns lived on the interest of their dowries. A house was rented and the nuns opened a boarding school. They received two novices, Catherine Wyse, a niece of Anastasia, and a postulant, Mary Pilkington. Difficulties arose and the nuns' legal title to their convent was questioned. The nuns could not find proof that there had ever been a Dominican convent of women in Waterford prior to their coming there. The matter was settled by a brief from Rome in 1742, legalising the nuns' position. However, the Waterford convent could not sustain itself and was dispersed in 1758 'for lack of funds'. The last Dominican nun in Waterford was probably Sr Catherine who was professed in 1749. One of the three nuns then remaining in Waterford went to the Dominican convent in Galway, the other two, 'because their dowries were too small, took shelter with their families in Waterford itself'.[16]

15. Fenning, H., *The Irish Dominican Province, 1698-1797* (Dublin: Dominican Publications, 1990) pp 152-53
16. H. Fenning, *The Irish Dominican Province*, pp 355-56

CHAPTER TWO

The Galway Origins of Channel Row

The Provincial Chapter of the Dominican Friars held in 1643, as we have read in the last chapter, approved and confirmed the Convent of Jesus and Mary Galway, as a monastery of the Order of Preachers under the jurisdiction of the Irish Provincial, who at the time was Father Terence Albert O'Brien. Fr Terence was present at the Provincial Chapter in 1643 and was appointed Bishop of Emly by the pope in 1647 but very soon fell into the hands of the Cromwellian soldiers after the siege of Limerick. He was captured while tending the sick in the city and Cromwell's son-in-law, Ireton, ordered that he be hanged. Terence died on the scaffold on 30 October 1651. Another Dominican priest, Fr Peter Higgins Prior of the Dominicans in Naas Co Kildare, had been hanged nine years previously on 23 March 1642. Both men are among the seventeen Irish martyrs beatified by Pope John Paul II in 1992. Not alone were religious men put to death in this era, laymen also suffered the death penalty – a reminder to us of the difficulties for all Catholics in Ireland during the seventeenth and eighteenth centuries and it gives us an idea of the political climate in which the Dominican nuns settled in Galway in what was then Tower Street, now St Augustine Street. They were very well aware of the dangers to which such a life-choice could expose them. Circumstances of war, plague, famine, siege, and finally the capitulation of Galway to the Cromwellian forces in April 1652, 'deprived [them] of the peace and security conferred on them by official approval'.[17]

The newly settled community heard continuously of the sufferings of their Dominican brethren and undoubtedly this caused them great stress and anxiety. They were not long waiting for trouble to come to their own door. In 1651 shortly before Fr Terence Albert O'Brien's death, the citizens of Galway expecting

17. R. O'Neill OP, *A Rich Inheritance, Galway Dominican Nuns 1644-1994* (Galway: Dominican Sisters 1994) p 10

a siege, fortified the town as well as they could. By September the blockade was complete but early in 1652 plague broke out and death and destruction were widespread. The nuns meanwhile gave whatever support they could to the needy and spent their time in prayer and penance for the relief of the suffering victims of the war. The city capitulated to the forces of Cromwell in April 1652 and for the nuns it meant they could no longer stay in their convent. They had two choices: go home to their families and probably abandon their religious life or go into exile and seek shelter in Dominican convents in Spain or elsewhere on the continent. Many of their Galway fellow-citizens and Dominican friars were forced to do likewise.[18]

Exile and Return

The Dominican friars were well acquainted with their Dominican brothers in Spain and other European countries. Many Irish Dominicans had been educated on the continent and Fr Gregory French negotiated with the Spanish Dominicans to take the Galway nuns into their convents. In 1652 four convents, Zamora, Toledo, Valladolid and Bilbao gave shelter to the fourteen Irish Dominican exiles. Twelve of the fourteen never saw Ireland again; two of them, Sisters Juliana Nolan and Mary Lynch were destined to play a major role in the reinstatement of the Galway Dominicans. Both Juliana and Mary were given a new home in the Dominican Convent of the Incarnation in Bilbao where the Spanish nuns had a school. It was a seaport town on a river estuary near the Bay of Biscay and was the capital of the Basque Country. This is a part of Spain which would be familiar to modern Irish tourists but to the two exiled nuns in 1652 it must have seemed a long way from home. It is an indication of the political realities of the time and of the close links of Ireland with Spain that King Philip IV paid four thousand *reales* for the two nuns' dowries to the convent in Bilbao. Juliana Nolan and Mary Lynch were remarkable women who settled happily into life in a Spanish convent for thirty-four years, be-

18. I am heavily reliant on the opening chapters of Sr Rose O'Neill's book, *A Rich Inheritance*, for the Galway background story of the Channel Row nuns.

came fluent Spanish speakers and Mary and probably Juliana taught in the school. Both were ready to sacrifice themselves once again in 1686.

In that year, the Irish Dominican provincial, Fr John Browne, requested both Juliana and Mary to go back to Ireland and re-sume Dominican life in Galway city. Even though the Stuarts had regained the throne of England in 1660-85, both the stability of the restoration and the political power of the Stuarts were un-certain as the nuns realised within a short time. Juliana and Mary landed in Galway in 1686 but they were coming home at a very dangerous time indeed, to an Ireland which would soon see King William of Orange take the throne and end the power of the Stuarts forever. The definitive battle between the forces of William and James was fought out at the River Boyne in 1690.

After 1690 trusting a Stuart, *'an rí thar sáile'* (the king over the water) for protection and restoration of their rights, had left the Irish Catholics worse off than they had been in the four years previously when Juliana and Mary arrived from Spain.[19] Protestant ascendancy was again restored and King James's going to France gave some substance to the hope of a return of the Stuarts and that Irish Catholic interests would be looked after in that event.

Their hope was that an heir of James II might one day return and reclaim the throne of England; this continuing hope was a threat to the English but a dim beacon of light to the Irish in this dark hour. The real truth was that whenever there was even a rumour of a Stuart returning, the established rulers in Ireland and the government in England became nervous. They in-creased the persecution and pursuit of the clergy and their sup-porters among the laity, including the nuns. Fines were imposed on those who harboured priests, either secular clergy or reli-gious. The fines ranged from £20 for the first offence, £40 for the second; the third offence carried the heaviest and most far-reaching penalty in its consequences, the forfeiture of lands, goods and chattels. This was the reality of life for Juliana and Mary as they began the difficult task of re-founding a convent

---

19. *'An rí thar sháile'* – an Irish phrase, 'the king over the sea'. It was a phrase used in an oblique reference to the Stuart king who had gone into exile in Europe.

and accepting and training girls who wished to become Dominicans. Add to this the fact that Juliana and Mary were no longer young; Juliana was seventy-five years of age and Mary about sixty and it could be said that they must have had a wonderful trust in the divine power of God, whatever about trusting in the political power of the Stuarts.

Williamite Persecution

From a house in the centre of Galway donated to them by the first Catholic mayor of the city, Sir John Kirwan, in 1686 the two nuns succeeded in building up a community in a well-organised convent where religious life was lived in a very strict manner. Gradually they took up again the religious observances 'in accordance with the rules and customs of the Order'.[20] Kirwan's Lane house was not built as a convent, but the returned exiles were determined that Dominican life would be lived as fully as possible. When numbers increased, the community rose for midnight matins in Advent and Lent and strict enclosure was observed. However, the peace and tranquility was not to last.

With the advent of William of Orange to the throne in 1689, further persecution of Catholics resumed; their friend and provincial, Fr John Browne spent over four months in prison in Galway and in 1698 there was mass banishment of the clergy. The Act (9 Will III, c.1) decreed:

> ... [all] popish archbishops, bishops, vicars general, deans, Jesuits, monks, friars and all other regular popish clergy and all Papists exercising ecclesiastical jurisdiction, shall depart out of this kingdom before the 1st May, 1698. If any of the said ecclesiastical persons shall be at any time after the said 1st May, 1698, within the kingdom, they and every of them shall suffer imprisonment, until he or they shall be transported beyond the seas; and if any person so transported shall return again into this kingdom, they and every of them shall be guilty of high treason and suffer and forfeit as in case of high treason [death and forfeiture of goods][21]

The soldiers invaded the nuns' cloister and the nuns were

20. R. O'Neill, *A Rich Inheritance*, p 14
21. M. Wall, *Ireland in the Eighteenth Century* (Dublin: 1989) p 9

scattered in the town staying with friends and relatives. There were other dispersals in the reign of Queen Anne; at these times the nuns were forced to flee into the countryside. They reassembled after some time but Juliana Nolan died in 1701 in her ninetieth year. She was indeed a valiant woman; both Juliana and her companion Mary Lynch deserve to have their memory honoured by posterity.

Mary Lynch was appointed prioress in January 1702 by the Dominican Provincial Fr Ambrose O'Connor. One of her community who was a novice during Juliana Nolan's last year was Mary Bellew. Mary Bellew made profession of vows in the hands of Mary Lynch on 2 November 1702. There were thirteen nuns in the community but the bad days were by no means over and uncertainty dogged them. The nuns were again dispersed in 1711 but by 1714 they were again together as a community. Their house was frequently invaded by soldiers searching for priests. Fr McDermott, a Dominican, who had been arrested and gaoled in Galway, asserted that the nuns had been dispersed three times during the months he had spent in prison. While he was in prison Fr McDermott requested the Master of the Order in Rome to find homes for thirty-nine Galway Dominicans in convents in France or Spain. He had good reason to make the request; in a letter dated 4 May 1714 Mayor Samuel Eyre writing to the Secretary of State in Dublin Castle states:

> I have made diligent search and dispersed the nuns that were in this town but now I am informed that they are gathering again and that ... if they be dispersed one day they may assemble again[22]

Eyre did not give up and neither did the nuns. In June of that year he issued more search-warrants for priests and said '[he] had again dispersed the nuns'. As a result of all this harassment the possibility of once again going to Spain was explored; six of the Galway nuns went to Madrid in 1717 but they failed to get a house for themselves. They were scattered among the Spanish convents and they never returned to Ireland.[23] This must have

22. R. O'Neill, *A Rich Inheritance*, p 20
23. H. Fenning, *The Irish Dominican Province, 1698-1797* (Dublin: Dominican Publications) p 77

been a devastating blow to those who remained in Galway, hop-
ing perhaps to join their Irish companions in Spain and live in a
convent of their own. Between the dispersal of 1652 and that of
1717, twenty Irish Dominican nuns went into exile in Spain and
in 1717 the nuns who remained in Galway were again sheltering
with friends in the city.

The then Provincial, Fr Hugh Callanan, suggested that some
of the nuns who had stayed in Galway should go to Dublin. The
Archbishop of Dublin, Dr Edmund Byrne (1707-23) had given
his consent to the Poor Clares in Galway to come to his archdiocese and they had already settled in Dublin in a convent in
Channel Row. Now Archbishop Byrne agreed to allow the
Galway Dominicans also to come to Dublin. All these factors,
the harassment, the failure to get a house in Spain, and the success of the Poor Clares in Dublin, must have influenced the
Galway Dominican nuns to put their trust in God and this time
instead of trusting the Stuarts, they trusted the Archbishop of
Dublin and were not disappointed. Unfortunately Archbishop
Byrne had suffered for his helping the Poor Clares to settle in
Dublin. In 1712, he along with one of his priests, Cornelius Nary
and the Franciscan Provincial, Fr John Burke were accused of
exercising ecclesiastical jurisdiction by bringing the Poor Clares

> [t]hat Unlawful Society of Popish Persons calling themselves
> Nuns from the town of Gallway to the City of Dublin ... con-
> trary to the laws of this kingdom ... wherefore we the Lords
> Justices and Council gave direction for apprehending them
> in order to their being examined and further proceeded
> against according to law; ... to the end therefore that the
> good laws made against Popish regulars may be put into due
> execution ... we the Lords Justices and Council do think fit
> by this our proclamation strictly do charge and command
> the Lord Mayor of the city of Dublin and all Justices of the
> Peace ... to use their utmost endeavours to take and appre-
> hend said John Burke, Dr Byrne and Dr Nary and so to com-
> mit them and every of them to safe custody.... Given 20
> September 1712[24]

24. *Dublin Intelligence*, Newspaper September 25 1712; See Appendix 1,
p 99

It is natural to ask how it was possible that the nuns should feel more secure in Dublin than in Galway; the most important factor at any given time in this period was the political situation in Dublin. Living in Dublin at the time was not as difficult for the nuns as living in Galway. Legally the Viceroy was the head of the Irish political establishment and was assisted in the discharge of his duties by various officials, among them the Lords Justices of whom the Lord Chancellor and the Primate of the Established Church were the most important. In the early decades of the eighteenth century these gentlemen, who frequently changed office, differed among themselves as to the severity to be used in the pursuit of Catholics.

> Sir Constantine Phipps, Lord Chancellor in the reign of Queen Anne persecuted nuns in Dublin and Galway but incurred the anger of the Irish House of Commons for not prosecuting a Dublin Jacobite bookseller with sufficient enthusiasm.[25]

To many followers of William of Orange, Jacobite booksellers posed more of a threat than nuns; these booksellers were propagandists openly supporting and encouraging the Stuart cause. In that respect the nuns in Dublin seem to have been under threat less frequently from the establishment than were their Galway counterparts. Another factor was that at the time, the majority of the citizens of Dublin belonged to the Established Church and felt secure in their own position. They did not feel threatened by a group of women, even if the women were nuns. The Penal Laws were not so rigorously enforced in Dublin, therefore, as in other parts of the country. In Dublin, tolerance and persecution of Catholics came in waves and the Archbishop of Dublin, Dr Edmund Byrne, was in turn able to attend a public debate with bishops of the Established Church in Trinity College while still being the subject of a proclamation calling for his arrest.[26] There seems to have been an uncomfortable climate of uncertainty rather than an immediate threat of active persecution in Dublin. These were the considerations which swayed both the

25. M. Craig, *Dublin 1660-1860, The Shaping of a City* (Dublin: Liberties Press 1952) p 126
26. P. Fagan, *The Second City* (Dublin: 1989) p 37

Dominican provincial, Fr Hugh Callanan and some of the nuns in Galway; the die was cast for the group of eight who agreed to take their chances and move to Dublin. The eight were: Mary Bellew, leader or prioress of the group, Julia Browne, Ellen [Elinor] Keating, Mary and Catherine Plunkett, Alicia Rice, Honoria Vaughan and Elizabeth Weever. We will try to establish the family background of these women and follow their lives in eighteenth-century Dublin.

CHAPTER THREE

Settling in Dublin

Fisher's Lane in Dublin, where Mary Bellew and her companions lived for a few months from March 1717, was north of the Liffey. The small warren of streets which included Fisher's Lane is today bounded by Mary's Lane to the north, Chancery Street to the south, Greek Street and Arran Street to the west and east respectively. Presentday St Michan's Street and the fruit market correspond roughly to the site of Fisher's Lane. Channel Row, where the Dominican nuns took up permanent residence in September 1717, was quite near Fisher's Lane and slightly to the north-west of it.[27] The convent to which they moved was in a more open place and was better suited to their purposes; it was leafy countryside and was not then regarded as part of the city. The name Channel Row was changed to North Brunswick Street in the mid-eighteenth century but it retained its original name in popular usage for many years after that. From the historian's point of view, it is more important to establish why the group of nuns from Galway chose that part of the city.

In the sixteenth century English Benedictine nuns settled in Brussels as 'a place of refuge and education for Catholic ladies whose religion was proscribed in England.'[28] They had houses in Pontoise, Dunkirk and Ypres. About 1680 the house in Ypres was allocated to the Irish nation, through the influence of two Irish members of the community, Dame Alexis M. Legge and Dame Mary J. Ryan. The community was henceforth known as 'the Irish Dames of Ypres' and Dame Ryan had visited Ireland

---

27. C. T. McCready, *Dublin Street Names, Dated and Explained* (Dublin: 1892) p 87; Ordnance Survey of Ireland, *Dublin Street Guide* (Dublin: 1995) p 36; Rocque's Map of Dublin 1757 has the convent on Channel Row clearly marked as 'Nunnery'.
28. T. King Moylan, 'The District of Grangegorman' part III, *Dublin Historical Record* Vol VII (Dublin: 1945) p 104; see Rocque's Map of Dublin, following page 64.

with the permission of the then Archbishop of Dublin, Dr
Russell, who promised ecclesiastical protection for a
Benedictine foundation in Dublin. In 1686 or 1687 the abbess of
the Ypres convent was Dame Mary Butler, a member of the family of the Duke of Ormond. Dame Butler was invited to make a
foundation in Dublin, an invitation which came indirectly from
King James II through his Lord Lieutenant, the Duke of Tyrconnell,
Richard Talbot.[29] In an article in the *Irish Ecclesiastical Record* in
1891, E. W. Beck has a long transcript of the royal charter given
by James II which in part says:

> James the II, by the grace of God, of England, Scotland and
> Ireland King … to all whom these presents shall come, greet-
> ing, know ye that we of our special grace … grant and constit-
> ute, ordain, declare and appoint that there shall be from time
> to time and at all times hereafter in our city of Dublin … a
> convent of nuns of the Order of St Benedict …[30]

The nuns came and at first lived for a short time in Ship Street,
close to Dublin Castle; afterwards they moved to the house in
Channel Row; they thought the time was favourable to them to
open a school in Ireland and allegedly King James was present at
the dedication of the convent in 1689. It is believed that later the
Williamite soldiers plundered the convent and the Benedictines
eventually returned to Ypres after the defeat of the Boyne and the
house in Channel Row became vacant. It was next used by the
Poor Clares when they came from Galway in 1712; they were invited by the parish priest Dr Nary, to make a foundation in St
Michan's parish but within three months of their arrival the convent was raided by the authorities and some sisters were arrested.
When the situation eased the Poor Clares returned and four
novices were professed but '[B]elieving that it would be safer if
they moved to a new location, the Poor Clares left Channel Row.'[31]
Sometime later they moved to 63 North King Street, where as the
same source writes, 'they took girls as boarders in an effort to
avoid detection'. The Channel Row convent was again vacant

29. T. King Moylan, 'The District of Grangegorman' p 105
30. E. W. Beck, *Irish Ecclesiastical Record*, May 1891 (Maynooth) p 412
31. Anonymous Booklet, *Bi-Centenary of St Clare's Convent, Harold's
Cross* (Dublin: 2004) p 4

until it was given to Mary Bellew and her community of
Dominicans in September 1717. The Duchess of Tyrconnell, the
wife of the Duke (Richard Talbot of Malahide), befriended both
the Poor Clares and the Dominicans and the Duchess died in 1730
in the Poor Clare convent in North King Street. The story of the
Channel Row house illustrates the type of involvement the Stuarts
and their supporters had with the Catholic cause and particularly
with the families of the Anglo-Irish who were faithful to James II
up to and beyond the Battle of the Boyne in 1690. This will be
borne out as the story of the Channel Row Dominicans unfolds.

Anglo-Norman Families, Channel Row and Oxmantown
Mary Bellew and most, if not all of her companions were of
Anglo-Norman ancestry. Their surnames bear witness to that:
Julia Browne, Ellen [Elinor] Keating, Alicia Rice, Mary and
Catherine Plunkett, Honoria Vaughan, Elizabeth Weever. The
records of the school in Channel Row give ample evidence that
the boarders who came to be educated by the Dominicans were
either nieces of the nuns themselves or very often were from
other Anglo-Norman families. The group of eight Dominicans
from Galway must have been very grateful to Lord Lieutenant
Talbot for allowing Mary Bellew to take over the convent in
Channel Row in 1717 and the Talbots of Malahide remained
friends with the nuns and were in regular communication with
them for many years. The holding taken over by the nuns 'con-
sisted of a dwelling house and a chapel, which were separate
buildings. The dwelling was a spacious four-storey building with
a garden and avenue attached'.[32] The area in which Channel Row
stood, known as Oxmantown, stretched as far as St Mary's
Abbey. This area was then outside the city boundary, an ancient
settlement of the 'Ostmen', as the Vikings were called. It was fert-
ile farming land well known for its orchards and sited not very
far from Cabra (where eventually the Dominican nuns were to
settle in 1819). In 1723 another house was leased and named in
the *Cabra Annals* as 'ye little house' and it is recorded that
£30.0s.0d was 'paid to Mr Knight for lace for ye little house.[33]
This is the first reference to any house other than the convent.

32. *Cabra Annals*, p 27
33. Ibid, p 35

A third house was acquired in 1730, rented from a Mr Weldon for £10 and which had several out-offices and was known as 'the Speaker's House' or 'ye back house', was thought to have been occupied by the Speaker of the House of Commons, Mr Ralph Gore when the parliament sat from September 1729 to April 1730.[34] The Irish parliament held its sessions in the Blue Coat School in Queen Street, founded in 1669 after the Stuart Restoration. The school was close to the convent and so the house was conveniently nearby. This house was on the opposite side to the road from the convent and was in the parish of St Michan's. The rent for the houses was paid at irregular intervals, whenever the nuns could get cash; sometimes they had to borrow the money to pay the rent. In 1726 there was a chapel, eight cells, novitiate, refectory, infirmary, two parlours, a pensioners' parlour and a wash-house. There were also eighteen standing beds in the pensioners' apartment. A big re-building of the convent from the ground up was done between 1747-50 at a cost of £1627-7-0. The accommodation was increased considerably to thirty-six rooms, besides five parlours, school, novitiate, infirmary, wash-house, dairy and kitchen.

The location of Channel Row had advantages for the nuns: the area north rather than south of the Liffey was more suited to a peaceful life as it was a distance away from Dublin Castle and the attention of government officials. It had the advantage of being near the Dominican friary sited on Bridge Street near the Liffey quays, close to where the Four Courts building is today. This ensured that the nuns would benefit from the ministrations of the priests; the friars would say Mass and administer the sacraments for them and be close at hand in time of danger. The nuns were also near the parish clergy as 'the old [Protestant] parish of St Michan's on the north side of the Liffey was, by act of parliament, divided into three parishes. The new parishes of St Michan's, St Paul's and St Mary's were the result and churches were erected on each of the two latter.'[35] The Catholic parishes St Mary's and St Paul's based on the civil parishes were created under Archbishop Byrne in 1707 and 1708 and the archbishop

34. T. King Moylan, 'The District of Grangegorman' part III, *D.H.R.* p 108
35. W. Harris, *The History and Antiquities of the City of Dublin* (Dublin: 1766, reprinted 1994) p 367

took advantage of this to appoint a parish priest in each of the civil parishes.[36] In time, the nuns' houses straddled two parishes, St Michan's and St Paul's; the disadvantage was they had to pay taxes for the upkeep of two Protestant churches: 'Paid a sess in the parish of St Paul £1.0.9d,' and 'paid ye parish clerk of St Michan's, £0'0s'9d'.[37]

Returning to the history of some of those families we find that the nuns succeeded in Channel Row for almost one hundred years but eventually had to yield to circumstances and move on to another location. From the evidence of the primary source materials, we know the community depended greatly on their own families to support them by sending their daughters to the school, with donations of money, and moral support.[38] Mary Bellew's family came from Barmeath not far from Drogheda in County Louth. The Bellews suffered from the upheavals of the seventeenth century when one of family, John Bellew of Lisrenny and Willistown, Co Louth was transplanted to Connacht. This was in consequence of his joining the Catholic Confederacy and participating in the rebellion of the 1640s. He was successful in regaining portions of his Louth holdings at the Restoration. John Bellew also retained the lands granted him in Galway where … 'his descendants were in possession of some 1,300 acres … The senior branch of the family, through his eldest son Patrick, continued to reside at Barmeath, Co Louth.'[39] Many other Anglo-Irish families, especially those from Fingal, took an active part in the rebellion of 1641. The names familiar to friends of Channel Row appear frequently in the accounts of the attacks from within the Pale: Talbot, Netterville, Barnewall, and Plunkett all sided with Eoghan Roe O'Neill against the Duke of Ormond and their loyalty to the Stuart cause was common knowledge.[40]

36. P. Fagan, *Dublin's Turbulent Priest* (Dublin: 1991) p 32
37. Dominican Archives, Cabra, *Account Book* No 4, August 1745
38. Dominican Archives, Cabra, *Channel Row Account Books*
39. K. Harvey, 'The Family Experience: The Bellews of Mount Bellew' in *Endurance and Emergence:Catholics in Ireland in the Eighteenth Century*, ed, T. P. Power and Kevin Whelan (Dublin: Irish Academic Press, 1990) p 176-77.
40. M. Ní Mhurchadha, *Fingal, 1603-60* (Dublin: Four Courts Press) 2005, see chapter 9 especially

This is the background from which Mary came; she showed remarkable leadership qualities immediately on taking over the Channel Row convent. She opened a boarding school for young ladies and a 'retirement home' for Catholic ladies in the very heart of Dublin in 1719 despite the penal laws' threat of fines and/or imprisonment. The direct descendants of Mary's family, the Honourable Bryan Bellew and his wife Rosemary are still living in Barmeath, Co Louth. It was confirmed by them that Barmeath was Mary's home though the house has been extended considerably and 'castellated' since her lifetime. Using the dates given in *Burke's Peerage* and comparing them with the family tree in possession of the Bellews, the evidence shows that Sir John Bellew, the second Baron of Barmeath, married in 1685.[41] Mary seems to have been the eldest in Sir John's family; her profession date is given as 1702 in Galway, when she was sixteen or seventeen years of age. This early age for profession was not unusual at the time. In fact, for all those who entered in Channel Row between 1720 and 1800, the average age at the time of their profession was sixteen years.

The family trees of the other members of the group of eight who came to Dublin in 1717 are not so easily accessible as the Bellews but we do have information about some of them. Julia Browne was a cousin of Mary Bellew; Julia's mother was a Bellew of the Barmeath family who married John Browne of the Neale, Co Mayo. This family of Browne was one of the 'tribes' of Galway established in Connacht from Anglo-Norman times. These families of the 'tribes' held on to their privileges and as recently as the early nineteenth century they asserted their right to elect the Catholic clergy of the city of Galway.[42] An ancestor of Julia's was sheriff of Mayo in the sixteenth century and later generations were Barons of Kilmaine; Julia'a father was taken prisoner on the 6 May 1689 at the siege of Derry. Julia's mother was his second wife and bore him eleven children, three sons, and eight daughters, of whom Julia was the eighth child. In 1998, a twentieth-century relative of Julia, John Lord Kilmaine,

---

41. I am grateful to The Honourable Bryan Bellew for allowing me access to the family papers. *Burke's Peerage*, p 237
42. T. P. O'Neill, *The Tribes and other Galway Families* (Galway: 1984) p 1

living in England, kindly supplied a paper with a synopsis of the last will of John Browne, Julia's father. In this paper there is a list of the daughters' names with the names of their spouses; in Julia's case it reads: *'Julia, qui devient religieuse'* (Julia who became a religious). This confirms her identity as being the Julia Browne of the Neale and of Channel Row. Julia Browne features later in this story of Channel Row as a strong-willed woman with great independence of mind.

Mary and Catherine Plunkett were close relatives (but not nieces as was sometimes alleged) of Saint Oliver Plunkett. The Plunkett family had long-standing connections with Co Louth and the territory of Fingal in north Co Dublin. When the nuns moved into Channel Row, Catherine Plunkett went to Belgium where she joined the convent of the English Dominicans there. It is thought perhaps that they may have had family connections in Brussels; we know very little of Mary Plunkett beyond the fact that her death is recorded in the Galway profession register under the date 24 June 1719.[43] Catherine spent five years in the convent in Brussels before being recalled to Ireland by the Dominican provincial to re-found the Dominican convent in Drogheda in 1722, known today as Siena Convent, Drogheda. Alicia Rice's father was Sir Stephen Rice, a prominent Jacobite who for a time was Baron of the Exchequer; he 'was among the Jacobites who suffered for their adhesion to the cause of James II'.[44] The Rices were of Welsh origin, (Rhys) and they had an estate in Dingle, Co Kerry. We have no certain knowledge of the families of either Honoria Vaughan or of Elizabeth Weever. Vaughan is also a Welsh name though there is a branch which stems from the Co Clare family of Mohan.[45] Ellen [Elinor] Keating's family name is one of the earliest hibernicised Anglo-Norman families who settled in south Leinster. They too were associated with the Jacobites; one of them was a notable figure in the parliament of 1689 but we have no evidence to link Ellen Keating with this particular branch of the family but it may not

---

43. Archives, Taylor's Hill Convent, *Register of Professions 1719*
44. E. MacLysaght, *Irish Surnames* (Dublin: 1957) p 257
45. E. MacLysaght, *Irish Families, their Names, Arms and Origins* (Dublin: 1985 Irish Academic Press) p 124

be too fanciful to think that she was related to them, though very distantly. The Weever family was also Anglo-Norman but no details of Elizabeth's immediate family have come down to us.

As already noted, the Channel Row Dominican nuns all had family backgrounds which had a pride in their heritage, who kept to their principles and had been proved loyal and faithful to their religious beliefs throughout the previous centuries. With such ancestry, it should not surprise us that Mary Bellew and her companions proved themselves capable of that same tenacity and independent thinking when they came to Dublin and opened their school in Channel Row. They must surely have had influential backing for their way of life and for their school both from their connections with the Catholic landed gentry in the Pale, and at times with people who had parliamentary and military positions in the time of the Stuarts. When the Stuart era was over, they managed to survive and prosper probably because their relatives had the benefit of the Articles of Limerick – unlike 'the native Celtic Race' who were disinherited.

> The Treaty of Limerick was signed on 3 October 1691 and had both military and civil articles. The civil articles were about protecting those Jacobites who chose to remain in Ireland. They also outlined how Catholics would be treated in an Ireland ruled by a Protestant monarch. Under the military articles, members of the Jacobite army could leave Ireland for France, along with their wives and children. Many chose to do so. Under the civil articles Jacobites who remained in Ireland were to be left in peace as long as they pledged allegiance to King William. They were allowed to keep their estates and property. Catholic noblemen were also permitted to carry arms. Despite this, the Penal Laws were still enforced and Irish Catholics were persecuted and the Treaty of Limerick was ignored.[46]

Rose O'Neill relates how as late as 1731 the Mayor of Galway made an order that 'all monasteries, friaries, nunneries should be suppressed' and that the final dispersal of the nuns in the Galway Dominican convent occurred towards the end of 1733.[47]

46. http://www.askaboutireland.ie
47. R. O'Neill, *A Rich Inheritance*, p 24

The Dominicans in Channel Row had their encounters with the authorities also and were brought to court at least on one occasion, but they never again had to flee their convent.

CHAPTER FOUR

The Channel Row Nunnery

The Dominican community in Channel Row, Dublin, was formally recognised by Letters Patent sent by the Master of the Order in Rome, Fr Antoninus Cloche. He allowed the dowries of those who had come from Galway to Dublin to be transferred to the Dublin convent. The document was dated 28 May 1718. As evidence that this was done, the Channel Row accounts for October 1719 state: 'received from Gallway in part of the pension £17.8s.0d', and again in January 1720: 'received from Gallway; pension/portion £35.0.0'. These acknowledgements were signed by Julia Browne, Eliza Weever and Ellen Keating. Catherine and Mary Plunkett were not among the nuns who took up residence in Channel Row so Mary Bellew and her five companions were then officially and legally established as a separate and autonomous community under the jurisdiction of the Master of the Order of Preachers.[48] In 1721 the two convents of Galway and Dublin were legally enabled to elect their own prioresses according to the laws and constitutions of the Order of Preachers.[49]

Mary Bellew and her community did not own the convent in Channel Row; the Penal Laws prohibited them from buying property but they had a lease on the house and paid rent to a Mr Geering who acted on behalf of Christ Church whose property it was in law. The transaction is recorded in *Account Book* No 1:

Mem. 1726, March 13th. Received from Mrs Mary Bellew the Sum of £24.10s.0d. together with the rent of £12.10s.0d stopped to Church for last Michaelmas rent and six pounds paid by my order to Mr John … [name illegible] making in all £42.10s now left in her hands to paye Christ Church last

48. *Cabra Annals*, p 22. Dominican Archives, Cabra
49. J. Hardiman, *The History of the Town and County of Galway* (Dublin: 1820) p 277 and following

Ladye Day rent, which with £12.10s when paid will make £55 this in full for a Year's rent due to me 25 of March last past, for her holding in Channelrow, Dublin.

Witness my hand this 15th of March, 1726. Richard Geering. Rent entire for X Church last Ladye Day. Rent due 25th March 1726.[50]

It is strange that the Dominicans rented the premises from this gentleman who was acting for the Protestant trustees of Christ Church who in turn were profiting from the illegal renting.

As already mentioned, Channel Row convent was rebuilt in 1748 by the Dominicans to its original design. There is a list of rooms mentioned in the *Account Books* which are designated by colour, 'ye yellow room; ye blew room', ye red room'. These rooms were occupied by the lady boarders, also called parlour boarders. Some ladies had personal maids and so had a 'suite' of rooms, probably two, maybe in a few cases even three rooms. The general impression is that the nuns were prosperous up to the fifth or sixth decade of the eighteenth century. They conducted their boarding school, looked after the parlour boarders and lived their religious life in common. Their daily routine included the recitation of the Divine Office, meditation, and other prayers which took up a considerable portion of their time. In essentials their life was not very different from the life of religious up to and beyond the Second Vatican Council in the 1960s but they were very dependent financially on their families.

Financial Dependence

The Articles of Limerick included a guarantee of 'security of life and property for Jacobite officers and soldiers remaining in Ireland and submitting to the new government'.[51] The families of the Channel Row nuns would have had resources, especially land, and they were in a position to help their nun-relatives financially. If the community was threatened by law, some of their friends may have been influential in pleading the nuns' cause. At the very least, they were able to provide dowries for their

50. *Channel Row Account Book* No 1
51. J. C. Beckett, *The Making of Modern Ireland 1603-1923* (London: 1966) p 148

daughters or sisters who entered the convent; these dowries and the interest from them gave the community some guarantee of financial viability, certainly during the early decades of their time in Channel Row. It is doubtful if any young girl without a dowry would have been accepted into the community in the early years of the eighteenth century.

From the account books it is evident that the nuns' dowries were paid in the form of bonds. Banking in Ireland at that time was based on a small number of family banks; only four names are listed as bankers in Dublin for the years 1733-36, Swift, Henry, Latouche/Kane and Fade.[52] The banking system as we know it today did not exist but, besides those noted in the Almanacks and Directories of the time, there were other small private institutions acting as bankers. The bonds given as dowry money were promises to pay certain sums or a guarantee of the interest on the agreed sum paid annually. At the end of *Account Book* No 1, for the years 1719-29, there is a list of bonds given to the community. The amount of the individual bond value varies from £25 to £500 and in total their value is £6,380 sterling. An entry for 23 May 1728 reads 'Sir Stephen Rice and others' bond to John Bodkin for payment of five hundred pds dated 25 [May]'. Mention of interest paid is frequent:

> Memorandum that I have settled accts wth Mr Brown this 3rd day of Augt. 1727 and that I have cleared and paid him in full of interest due on my bond to Mr Michael Bellew ye 2nd day of June last.

> Recd from John Kelly Esq. ye sum of three pds wch Sum is to be pd towards entering judgmt upon Donnigh and Jo Kelly Esqs. Bond to ye Honble Elizabeth Burke of 400 pds Sterl For ye payment of 200 pds ster Bond and Warrant bears date the 3rd day of Augt 1727.

> Memorandum that I've settled accts With my Bror this 14th day of August 1727 and yt I've recd all interest due to me on his Bond & Warrt to ye 12 of ye month 1727.
> Signed: Rosa ffarrelle.[53]

---

52. *Watson's Almanac 1733-36* (Dublin: 1736)
53. *Account Book* No 2

Rosa Farrell was a member of the community at that date.

In her book *Sisters in Arms*, Jo Ann McNamara says that 'female monasticism had depended on generous subsidies from aristocratic donors, usually nuns themselves or their relatives.'[54] While it would not be fair to equate the Irish nuns with the aristocratic families on the continent, there is a certain parallel in their reliance on their families to subsidise their finances. A more detailed account of the function of the bonds will be given in a later chapter.[55] The Channel Row nuns earned the main part of their living through their boarding school and the parlour boarders' pensions and are cited by Jo Ann McNamara as an example of nuns who supported themselves by educating young women.[56] Nevertheless there are many entries in the account books of Channel Row which indicate they also were the recipients of donations in kind, church plate and gifts of money, mostly small amounts. Even on occasion they borrowed money from friends and family. The gifts in kind from relatives which were substantial tended to be gifts of church plate. In an inventory dated 27 April 1729, for the church alone, the following are some of the items noted:

Four large plate candlesticks £50.0.0
Four smale plate candlesticks £10.0.0
one plate lamp one plate thurible [censer]
Two plate chalices One plate ciborium [vessel for Communion Hosts]
One Silver Branch candlestick
One pair of large plate candlesticks.[57]

The silver branch mentioned was an eight branch chandelier surmounted by a silver dove and made by John Hamilton in Dublin in 1729. Hamilton had a shop in Ormond Quay, not far from Channel Row; he was a leading silversmith in the first half of the eighteenth century and was elected master of the

54. J. A. K. McNamara, *Catholic Nuns Through Two Millenia* (Harvard: 1996) p 527
55. See Chapters 6 and 9 below
56. J. A. K. McNamara, *Catholic Nuns*, p 528
57. *Account Books* Nos 1 and 4. See illustrations following page 64.

Goldsmiths Company in 1714.[58] The chandelier was given as a gift to Julia Browne during her term of office as prioress and her family also gave four baroque altar candlesticks to the convent in 1719.[59] The quality and number of such gifts is evidence that the families from which the nuns came were in very comfortable circumstances. The money gifts are entered individually from time to time and occur throughout the books:

February 1729 Rd in charity from Mrs Daly Blake £2.0.0.
Rd in charity from Mrs Mapus Burn £1.3.0.
1745, 'Recd in charity from Mrs Daly £1.02.09[60]

All this financial and material support was given to the community up to the last quarter of the eighteenth century but later on their families were no longer able to help them and the nuns' dependence on outside sources proved disastrous for the community in the long term.

The ministry which the nuns favoured and carried out in Channel Row was undoubtedly their school and the education which they gave to the girls who came to them. Many of the names of their pupils as recorded in the account books are evidence that they were members of the nuns' own families and friends. The same applies to the parlour boarders. Lady Tyrconnell, her daughters, Ladies Dillon and Kingsland and Mrs Browne, who may have been a relative of Julia Browne, are all mentioned as having lived in the house as benefactors. The Poor Clare nuns who were in Dublin at this time also had parlour boarders, so it would appear that there was a demand for accommodation for ladies, whether widowed or single, who were unable to live in a family setting and who could afford to pay rent or, as they called it, a 'pension' to the nuns.[61] In the society of the day, many families were concerned with holding on to their estates to forge marriage alliances which would ensure that the land remained in the family. For the daughters of these houses it was desirable that they too should 'marry well', meaning that they

58. J. McDonnell, ed, *Ecclesiastical Art of the Penal Era, Maynooth Bicentenary* (Maynooth: 1995) Exhibit no 37
59. *Account Books* Nos 1 and 4
60. *Account Book* No 2
61. H. Concannon, *The Poor Clares in Ireland* (Dublin: 1929) p 96

would marry into a family of at least equal status with their own. In some cases this social engineering resulted in unmarried daughters, or daughters who were not marriageable, being obliged to leave the family home to make way for their brother's bride. Channel Row provided an alternative home where these single ladies could reside with dignity and have a good social life according to the norms of their era.

CHAPTER FIVE

Community Life in Channel Row
Early Years

From the time of the foundation of the Order, Dominicans have had a participative system of government. Saint Dominic in 1215 sought approval from Rome for his group of a flexible system of government. They had come together to preach the Gospel to the people of Languedoc in southern France. The fourth Lateran Council held in the same year had decreed that 'anyone wishing to found a new religious order must adopt for it some existing rule.'[62] In deciding to adopt the rule of Saint Augustine, Dominic and his followers chose this particular rule because it did not prescribe any detailed regulations but laid down general principles. That gave the new Order scope to write constitutions which were adaptable and could be changed if and when circumstances demanded. Any major change in the constitutions was and is decided by the highest authority in the Order, which is the general chapter composed of delegates elected from each province. The general chapter elects the Master of the Order who is bound to carry out the ordinations of the chapter and is accountable to it. Each province in turn elects its provincial and each priory elects its prior. This form of organisation for religious was innovative at the time and served Dominic's purpose of participative government and mobility for the mission of preaching.[63] He had founded a convent for women in Prouillhe not far from Toulouse and in the early centuries each cloistered convent, while under the authority of the Master of the Order, elected its own prioress. The Master of the Order usually delegated the general responsibility for the nuns to the local Provincial or to another priest of the province.

When Mary Bellew and the group came to Dublin in 1717 she

---

62. S. Tugwell, *The Way of the Preacher* (London: 1979) p 5
63. V. Koudelka, *Dominic*, ed and trs S. Tugwell (London: 1997) pp 43-45

was regarded as the leader either by selection or force of personality but she was formally elected prioress in 1721 and was assisted in the government of the convent by a house council. The authorisation for this election came from a general chapter in Rome:

> We grant that the Convents of our Nuns who live in the cities of Dublin and Galway may elect for themselves Prioresses according to our holy constitutions and Laws, and we wish that the aforesaid Convents be incorporated with, and joined to, our Order, and be subject to the Provincial of Ireland for the time being.[64]

The names signed to the accounts up to 1723 are Julia Browne, Ellen Keating, Honora Vaughan, and Eliza Weever but all the receipts are in 'Mrs Bellew's name. Presumably these four, with Mary Bellew, formed the house council. In September 1723 Catherine Cruise's name was added; she and Rose Farrell were the first to be received into the Dublin community. The function of the house council is to advise the prioress on all issues of importance affecting the community and its wellbeing; there are definite matters about which the prioress must consult her council and for which she is accountable to them. In this way, there are certain restrictions on the prioress's government. In the matter of reception of novices and their profession as full members of the community, the whole community would have had a vote.

During Mary Bellew's period of leadership, the nuns arrived in Dublin, resided in Fisher's Lane for six months from March to September 1717 and then moved into Channel Row, the spacious four-storey building with a garden and avenue attached.[65] The design of the convent was interesting – small details tell their own tale: the entrance door to the chapel was not facing directly on to the street but it was placed discreetly at the side to disguise the fact that there was a chapel inside. The nuns risked penalties if it were known they had Mass celebrated in their convent. The doorway was very narrow but as King Moylan says: 'quite wide

64. T. de Burgo, *Hibernia Dominicana*, (Cologne: 1762) p 352
65. Typescript of first draft of *Cabra Annals* p10.

enough for the Dominicans to drive a coach-and-four through an Act of Parliament long before Daniel O'Connell coined the phrase'.[66] The chapel was a separate building and as custom required at the time, the entrance was at the side:

> In some parts of Ireland it may be noticed that the churches stand outside the town, and investigation would probably reveal that in most cases a site in the town itself was refused by the landlord or by the corporation. Where chapels existed in the eighteenth century they were usually to be found in back streets, and had neither steeple nor bell nor any outward sign which might give offence to Protestants.[67]

In her role as leader, Mary succeeded in putting the community on a firm footing in Dublin, with both papal approval and recognition that the convent had the right to elect its own prioress; her convent was accepted formally as part of the Dominican Order. The boarding school opened in October 1719 and the nuns accepted some ladies as parlour boarders. By the end of her term of office Mary Bellew's health was poor; in a long list of medicines bought from the apothecary the following appears:

> 12 papers cordial powder, Mrs Bellew (a heart stimulant)
> A Mixture for Mrs Bellew
> The purge for Mrs Bellew

Mary's heart condition was evidently giving cause for concern and there follow entries for money paid to the doctor for Mary who may have been prescribed 'country air', that is a period of convalescence in some eighteenth-century equivalent of today's nursing homes. As evidence of this there are references to 'Going to the country' in the account books as an expense item, when money was paid for lodgings and expenses in Finglas. Finglas is today part of the city of Dublin, having large twentieth-century housing estates, but in the eighteenth century it was 'out in the country', and belonged civically to a larger area known as Fingal, in north Co Dublin. In the eighteenth century Fingal was 'a centre for the Dublin gentry who ensured

---

66. T. King Moylan, 'The District of Grangegorman', *Dublin Historical Record*, Vol VII, 1945 p 109
67. M. Wall, *Collected Essays*, p 51

that their estates were adequately accommodated by the road network'.[68] A peerage title as Earl of Fingall (*sic*) was created in 1628 by King Charles I and granted to Lucas Plunkett, Baron of Fingall.[69] His wife, Elizabeth O'Donnell of Tyreconnell became the first Countess of Fingall and the Plunketts had a three storey tower house in the area. We must bear in mind that the Channel Row nuns had close family ties with many of the Catholic gentry in north Co Dublin, Louth, and Meath and there is a possibility that some of the community might have gone to their relatives to recuperate after illness. Lady Fingall is mentioned as being a patron of the convent and the Plunkett family had lands in the area. Over the centuries Fingal included as it does today, Howth, Swords, Blanchardstown, and other areas north of the city. Today it has regained its autonomy with its own local government structure.

Mary's stay in Finglas did not restore her health. Shortly after the entry in the account books, another entry reads: 'paid for a litter to carry home Mrs Bellew'. Her death is recorded on 24 August 1726 and she was buried in St James's churchyard in James's Street Dublin, not far from Channel Row. St James's Protestant Church was built in 1707 and its burial ground was one of the oldest in what is now the inner city. With Bully's Acre in Kilmainham and St Kevin's in Camden Row, it was the burial ground most used by Catholics during the penal times and is marked in Rocque's map of 1750.[70] St James's graveyard was renovated through a FÁS programme in 1987 but no trace or marker remains of the old graves. There is documentation about the burial places of some of the Channel Row nuns in the archives of the Church of Ireland College of Education in Rathmines.

With the exception of Alicia Rice, each of the other founding members of the community became prioress, one might say almost in turn, between 1726 and 1738. It is difficult to interpret what may have been the reason for these serial elections. It could be taken as a sign that the community saw the office of prioress

68. Finglas Environmental Heritage Project, *Finglas Through the Ages* (Finglas 1991) p 1

69. http://en.wikipedia.org/wiki/Fingal

70. V. Igoe, *Dublin Burial Grounds and Graveyards* (Dublin: Wolfhound Press, 2001) pp 241-249

as an honour to be bestowed on the more senior members and
therefore voted for each one in turn; it could be that each in turn
declined to be re-elected or that the community did not wish
any one person to have more than one term of office. Why was
Alicia Rice never elected and why does her signature never appear in the account books? Considering that she was the daughter of a baron of the exchequer, her education must have been
equal to that of the other ladies. Ill health may be one explan-
ation or perhaps an inability to take responsibility for running
an establishment as big as Channel Row. We do not know the
answers to these intriguing questions; one can only speculate.
Honora Vaughan did have a second term but not until 1750 and
she died in office in 1753.[71]

The Julia Browne Story

The most colourful character among the six foundresses was undoubtedly Julia Browne, the second prioress in Channel Row
from 1726-1729. In John Kilmaine's document already mentioned, the status of the Brownes of the Neale was set out.[72] They
are said to be the first family of Anglo-Norman descent to settle
in the country.[73] Julia's father Sir John was the third baron of
The Neale. His first wife died three months after the marriage
and Sir John's second marriage was to Julia Bellew of Barmeath,
(an aunt of Mary Bellew). Julia Browne's father was made a prisoner at the siege of Derry 1689 and abandoned the army of King
James II after the defeat of Aughrim 1691. He had eleven children, eight girls and three boys, Julia being the eighth child. She
was made of stern stuff and proved she could withstand many
disappointments without giving up hope. She was professed in
Galway on 27 December 1712 and by the time she was elected
prioress in Channel Row she had been in religious life for at
least fifteen years. She had the experience of the move to Dublin
and of settling into the daily life as lived in a convent with a
boarding school. During her term of office as prioress, there
were great signs of business and progress in the life of the com-

71. *Cabra Annals* (first draft) pp 7 and 24
72. Cabra Archives: Document re Brownes of the Neale, Co Mayo
73. htpp://mayo-ireland.ie/mayo/towns/CgCrssTN.htm

munity. The funds increased from £4,730 to £5,080 – not a great amount by our modern standards but at least the nuns were not in debt. The number of pupils increased and it was at this time that the second house was acquired and work was carried out on the chapel and the nuns' choir. The second house was a smaller dwelling and was rented from a Mr Deering at a yearly rent of £15. It is mentioned in the account books as 'ye Back House' but more frequently as 'ye Next House'. All this points to the period of Julia Browne's administration as successful and progressive but, according to the *Cabra Annals*,

> on being released from office in the year 1729, Mrs Julia Browne, on account of her health, and with the sanction of the Master General, Master Thomas Ripoll, went over to Belgium to the Dominican convent at Brussels, founded for English nuns ... She continued in Belgium until 1740, when she returned once more to Dublin, where she died in 1747.[74]

This brief and censored version of Julia Browne's life gives us no clue as to what had happened to Julia between 1729 and 1747. The only published full account I know of Julia's 'adventures' in Belgium is that of Hugh Fenning in his scholarly and meticulously researched work on the seventeenth century Irish Dominicans.[75] The indirect connection between the Channel Row Dominicans and the convent of English Dominicans in Brussels has been referred to in a previous chapter. It is probable that over the years there was some intermittent communication between the three communities of Channel Row, Brussels and Siena Convent Drogheda where Catherine Plunkett settled after her time in the Belgian convent. Julia Browne made some connection with that community when her term of office as prioress was concluded in Channel Row and with permission, she and a companion, Mary O'Daly, spent some time with the English Dominicans in Brussels before going for a period to 'take the waters' near Liege. In the autumn of 1730 the Brussels community was due to elect a prioress; Julia had 'made so favourable an impression on her

74. *Cabra Annals*, pp 42-43
75. H. Fenning, *The Irish Dominican Province, 1698-1797* (Dublin: Dominican Publications 1990) pp 158-163 and 178-180
76. Chapter 3 p 28

hosts that they elected her prioress of their convent'.[77] Julia accepted and took up office for the usual term of three years. At some stage Julia indicated that she would like to be officially assigned to the Brussels community and be affiliated to the English group of Dominicans. Her ambitions went further than that as we shall see.

Julia's Dream
The continued harassment of the nuns in Galway showed that the bad times were not yet over. They were once more expelled from their convents and dispersed in 1732; not alone the Dominicans, but the Augustinians and Franciscans were also expelled. Eight Irish bishops petitioned the Archduchess Maria Elizabeth, governess of the Austrian Netherlands (modern Belgium and Luxemburg) that a refuge be set up for the Irish nuns in Belgium which was within the archduchess's domain. Julia Browne's proposal was that she should set up such a house in Belgium and take some of the English Dominicans from the Brussels convent with her. Julia had in mind that the Channel Row community might use it should they be obliged to flee from Dublin and the 1732 episodes showed she had real reason to fear that the period of persecution of religious in Ireland was not by any means a thing of the past.

The Brussels Dominican community was not in favour of Julia's plan and so it did not then materialise. As the time for the election of a prioress in the Brussels convent came in 1733, the English community began to realise that Julia Browne might lead them along paths which they did not wish to tread and they feared she might be re-elected. Julia obviously had some supporters among the community. There was an impasse; the majority 'refused to proceed to a fresh election until Julia Browne was safely out of the house.'[78] It should be said that the English nuns would have had serious difficulties with Julia's scheme. Should it fail, the financial consequences could be disastrous; if some of the Brussels community joined Julia in a new convent, they feared they would then be obliged to hand over the dowries of

77. H. Fenning, *The Irish Dominican Province*, p 158
78. Ibid

those who went with Julia, as the Galway nuns had had to hand over the dowries for Channel Row. Hugh Fenning puts the response of the Brussels nuns in plain terms: 'It is not surprising that Julia was politely told to manage the refuge herself.'[79] We now see how determined and tenacious a person Julia Browne could be; Fenning refers to her as 'a woman of high resource'. Not only was she highly resourceful but she now had friends in high places:

> [T]he cardinal-archbishop of Malines brought her in his own coach to a Benedictine monastery where the nuncio permitted her to remain until such time as her business was concluded. She owed this high patronage to a recommendation from Hugh MacMahon, archbishop of Armagh who had played a large part in the foundation of the Dominican monastery [for nuns – Siena Convent] in Drogheda.[80]

Help from High Places

Julia's next supporter was no less a personage than the Archduchess Maria Elizabeth who was the sister of the Holy Roman Emperor Charles VI. The emperor issued an edict on 2 June 1734 setting out the conditions under which Julia would be allowed to found her refuge in Brussels. The substance of these conditions is set out below:

> a) the nuns should name the location in which they wished to establish their refuge
> b) they would be responsible for legal expenses in buying the property
> c) their establishment should never be a charge on the town; the religious should establish in advance that they had sufficient means to provide for the needs of the community
> d) the number of religious should never exceed that which Archduchess Maria Elizabeth, governess of the Austrian Netherlands, considered appropriate. If a novice were received, [the religious] should provide for her maintenance.
> e) the religious should never seek exemption from taxes or other charges

79. H. Fenning, *The Irish Dominican Province*, p 160
80. Ibid

f) the religious should never open a school nor accept as boarders or lodgers, any citizen of the Netherlands.[81]

These were rigorous conditions but nothing daunted, Julia sought help from the Archbishop of Malines who helped her to find a suitable house with a garden in Brussels for £600. She herself made a payment of £200 on the property and requested the Channel Row community to pay the balance and to send her six nuns from the Dublin community to be part of the new Irish/Brussels community. Julia meantime had also gained the support of the Master of the Order, Fr Thomas Ripoll. He gave his consent in September 1734 and requested the prior of Louvain, Dominic Brullaughan, to support her also. Julia set out for Ireland, no doubt confident that with the backing of all these high-ranking people, she would have all her requests granted by the Channel Row community. The prior of Louvain, Dominic Brullaughan, mindful that the Master of the Order had requested his help for Julia, escorted her to Dublin. Not alone had Julia now got the Holy Roman Emperor, an Archduchess, the Master of the Order, and the prior of Louvain on her side; she soon added to the list two Dominican bishops, Bishops Stephen Mac Egan of Meath and Michael MacDonagh of Kilmore. The Channel Row nuns would not be persuaded that they needed a house in Belgium which they had never sought to buy and which would tie them into conditions which they might find hard to accept and fulfil. They unanimously refused to give Julia the required £400 and stated that they had no intention of going to Brussels unless they were forced to leave Ireland through persecution.

John Kilmaine's interpretation of the Browne family papers which holds Julia's father's will written in 1700, is that John Browne left £300 to each of his daughters. This £300 was to be paid yearly from the rents arising from the family estates.[82] Julia then had her dowry in the safe-keeping of her brother and she now decided to use £150 to help with her new foundation in

81. H. Fenning, *The Irish Dominican Province*, p 161 (loosely translated from the French as given in the text)
82. *Cabra Archives*, Region of Ireland collection. Copy of the Browne Papers

Brussels. The Channel Row nuns however, were not in favour of allowing her to use the money. They held that the money should be transferred to them as it was originally intended as Julia's dower money from the Galway community. Again the master of the order intervened on Julia's behalf. He gave it as his opinion that if Galway could give over seven dowries to Channel Row, then Channel Row should give up this one dowry to Julia. This piece of encouragement made Julia all the more determined to pursue her course. Hugh Fenning comments: 'the whole project was thus opposed by the very nuns in whose name and for whose sake it had been broached'.[83] Julia's next move brought her back to Brussels in 1736, this time finding lodgings with the Canonesses of St. Augustine at Berlemont and having as companion Sr. Joseph Compton from the Dominican community in Brussels. The English community objected to this very strongly and the master of the order refused Sr. Joseph permission to leave her community. Julia then got a papal decree in August 1737 permitting Sr. Joseph to go with her to the new 'refuge' but still without the consent of the English community. Again the Archbishop of Malines hastily came to the rescue, providing a coach to bring Sr. Joseph to join Julia.

Disapproval and Disappointment
At this stage the Channel Row nuns tried once more to stop Julia and asked the Master of the Order, Thomas Ripoll, to intervene. Ripoll again sided with Julia, saying she had been unjustly treated and that she had now got what she most strongly insisted on, the money (£150) to buy a house for the refuge. Yet another ally had sprung up to defend Julia; this time it was an English priest Francis Goddard, administrator of the nunciature in Brussels. He sided with her against the Irish Provincial and the Channel Row nuns. June 1737 saw Julia Browne in a rented house with, it is said, three of her nieces. She fitted out the house with a grille and a chapel costing £500. This did not include the cost of decorating the chapel; the Cardinal-Archbishop of Malines had that done for her, under the supervision of his secretary. Two Galway nuns were given permission to join Julia in 1737, Srs

---

83. H. Fenning, *The Irish Dominican Province*, p 162

Mary and Elizabeth Browne. Mary went but Elizabeth never left
Galway. By the summer of 1738, Julia Browne, Sr Joseph
Compton of the English community in Brussels and Sister Mary
Browne of Galway were living in the rented house in Brussels.
They were joined in July 1738 by Sr Evangelist O'Kelly from
Galway who was appointed prioress by the Master of the Order
in 1739. The 'pioneers' of the refuge had little money left. 'There
was not much room, but they tried to make a start by receiving
'pensioners' or boarding pupils.'[84] The pensioners were probably
the equivalent of the 'parlour boarders' in Channel Row, ladies
who were paying guests and resided in the convent with, but
apart from, the nuns. This state of affairs did not last very long.

The Return of the Prodigal Daughter
At Christmas 1739 the Irish provincial, John Fotrell, made a visitation in the refuge in Brussels. He did not get a favourable impression of life in the community. The few students they had
withdrew to the English convent in January 1740. Sr Evangelist,
the prioress, had lost confidence in Julia Browne. The situation
was not a happy one for Julia even though her longed for Irish
refuge in the Austrian Netherlands had been partially achieved.
Money was scarce. Julia would not, nor possibly could not, buy
the house outright until she had proved that the refuge would
succeed. There were only two spare rooms and Sisters Joseph
Compton and Mary Browne would not under any circumstances allow pensioners in the house. Thomas Ripoll, Master of
the Order, refused to allow them to take novices. This must have
been a bitter blow to Julia who had her heart set on making a
success of the Brussels foundation. Discord set in among the
small community. Fr Thomas Ripoll kept his faith in the project
and insisted that the nuns should set up a boarding school
which had been the primary aim of the foundation and, as the
Queen of Portugal had supported this idea, Fr Ripoll agreed
with Fr Fotrell that Sr Mary Browne who 'would not or could
not teach', should go back to Galway and two other nuns
Catherine Lynch and Elizabeth Browne should come out and
help to set up the school. Sr Evangelist had had enough and she

84. H. Fenning, *The Irish Dominican Province*, p 145

insisted on returning to Galway; Fr Ripoll 'had not the heart to say no.'[85]

Mary Browne set out for Antwerp and thence to Galway. Julia Browne, the instigator of the whole expedition, was left alone to see her dream world collapsing around her. Eventually in autumn 1740, she left Brussels for the last time. On her way home she stayed with her brother in Paris for a short time and was in London by November 1741. From there she returned to the monastery in Channel Row Dublin where she died in March 1747. The man who had stood by her all through this difficult period, the Master of the Order Thomas Ripoll, was deeply disappointed and regretted most of all 'that the opposition of her own Dominican brothers and sisters in Ireland had caused Julia's plan to fail'.[86] It has to be said that the political opposition to nuns and friars in Ireland was not at all as strong in the 1740s as it had been in the first thirty years of the eighteenth century and hence a refuge on the continent of Europe for religious fleeing persecution was no longer necessary.

85. H. Fenning, *The Irish Dominican Province*, p 179
86. Ibid

CHAPTER SIX

Finances

Considering that lack of finance and gaining access to part of
her dowry was a problem for Julia Browne, it is interesting in
the twenty-first century to learn through research how the system
of dowries apparently worked in the mid-eighteenth century. In
chapter 4 above it is indicated that the dowry system was an important element of income for the community in Channel Row.
There was of course the income from the boarding school fees
and the so-called 'pensions' which the parlour boarders paid for
their board and lodgings but that income might rise and fall de-
pending on the numbers of school boarders and parlour boarders at any one time. The nuns' security came from having a steady
income from the bonds. Usually these were in the name/s of the
father or brother of the newly professed person and an account
of the bonds and the interest accruing from them was kept on
the receipts' side of the ledger. The interest on the bonds was
given every quarter or half yearly. The initial entry would read:
'Sir Stephen Rice, his bond to his daughter Alicia Rice, £500.'[87]
The interest on the bond would then be paid to the nuns according to the arrangements made between the original donor of the
bond and the community. The nuns held the actual paper bonds
in the convent in the 'depositum' or convent safe. There is an
oval shaped wooden box marked 'bonds' in the archives in
Cabra dating from this time. It seems in some cases at least that
the capital sum was kept by the donor.

One of the oldest documents we have in the Cabra archives
is part of one such legal document which gives 4 May 1722 as
the date of a bond or bonds given to the daughters of Hugh
Reilly [Reily] of Co Westmeath. These two daughters, Mary and
Jane Reilly were in school in Channel Row and later entered the
convent there. The legal document refers to a bond given by

their father Hugh Reilly and dated 4 May 1722 for the sum of £400 'conditioned for payment of the principal of £200 at the interest rate of 6 per cent per annum on a certain day therein mentioned.' The last portion of the document still extant mentions that both Mary and Jane Reilly 'went to reside in and become members of a Society of Females then established in Brunswick Street'.[88] It further stated that Jane assumed the name of Catherine on entering the convent and that she and Mary had received the interest on the bond until the day of their deaths. Mary Reilly died in 1749.[89] Members of the Reily/Nugent family are still in residence in Ballinough, Co Westmeath and have been helpful to us in researching material for this book.

Donations in kind were frequently given; the Brownes and the Bellews were generous benefactors of the Channel Row community. The Brownes gave presents of large plate candlesticks and other donations and the Bellews over the years had given candlesticks, a Holy Communion paten and thurible (censer).[90] Sir Edward Bellew had an organ installed in the chapel in Channel Row. The bonds and funds of 'the Family' (as the community was called) are stated at the close of each prioress's term of office from 1726 when Mary Bellew ended her three years as prioress, to 1825 when the community had been in Cabra for five years. The dowries from Galway do not seem to have been transferred to Dublin until 1724 or 1725. The yield from the bonds was at its highest between 1735 and 1759, yielding an average of about £1,500 per annum. The fortunes of the community fell steeply in the last decades of the eighteenth century leaving them with very little income as sadly will be shown in a later chapter.

Besides the families of the nuns, there were others who helped to finance the Channel Row community over the years: the Duke of Tyrconnell, Lord Talbot of Malahide and particularly his wife, the Duchess of Tyrconnell, one of the parlour boarders for some time were generous supporters. Lord and Lady Dillon, were also generous with their donations. The Lord Dillon men-

88. Channel Row was renamed Brunswick Street, 1766
89. Cabra Archives, Legal document fragment beginning with 'Jane Reilly ... bond or obligation ....'
90. List in Cabra archives

tioned in the account books was probably identical with the Governor of Galway in 1691 at the time of the Battle of Aughrim. In the account books also there is a list of these titled people whose daughters were in the boarding school or who were themselves parlour boarders.

Lord Mayo (Burkes) 2 daughters
Lord Kenmare (Brownes) 1 daughter
Lord Trimleston (Barnwalls) 2 daughters
Lord Riverston (Nugents) 2 daughters
Lord Dunsany (Plunketts) 2 daughters
Lady Cavan 1 daughter
Lady Rice 1 daughter
Viscount Netterville 2 daughters

Taxation

The taxation levied on Dubliners in the eighteenth century was often of a penal nature and the nuns no less than anyone else were affected by them. The Protestant ministers in each parish got tax money from the Catholics for their own upkeep, the upkeep of their church and their clerk. Besides these 'Protestant' taxes, there was a lengthy list of others payable by the citizens; the nuns have noted their own payment over the years:

Grand Jury cess	£1.09s.0d.
Minister mony in St Paul's	£1.04s.0d.
Cess for workhouse and foundling	£1.09s.0d.
Paid harth mony	£3.10s.0d
Paid minister and watch mony half a year	£2.03s.0d
Paid Grand Jury cess for transporting felons	£0.00s.6d
Paid lamp mony	£1.02s9d
Paid a year's minister's mony in St Michan's parish	£2.08s.0d
Paid a Grand Jury cess for repairing churches	£2.06s.0d
Paid ye parish clerk of St Michan's	£0.00s.9d
Paid the Bradoge cess	£0.18s.0d[92]

---

91. Hardiman, *History of Galway,* p 156
92. Cabra Archives, *Account Book* No 1 Channel Row. In quotations from the account books the spelling is as in the original entries

We note that minister's money was paid both to St Paul's and St Michan's parishes as the nuns held houses in both. The Bradoge cess was a tax on the local river. There was no centralised sanitation system in the early years and at times, 'paid a man to clean out the dirt hole' was the equivalent of cleaning out the sewers.

> The old city had been built around an unfortunate little river called the Poddle, which for centuries cleansed the city, serving as a natural sewer with innumerable privies draining into it. The Bradogue river performed a similar cleansing service on the North Side.[93]

It must have been galling for Catholics to have a tax levied on them for transporting 'felons'. Very often these felons may have been relatives, neighbours or friends who transgressed some of the penal laws against the Catholic religion. In later years new taxes were added, there was a paving tax, a pipe water tax, a police tax, a window tax; all these were paid in the 1790s. Modernisation has its own price.

One of the items which appears quite often in the books is, 'paid in charity for ye prisoners'; these donations were given to priests and other people in prison and who were known to the nuns. Conditions in the prisons were appalling. There were two prisons on the south side of the Liffey in the eighteenth century: one was the Black Dog, as the Marshalsea prison was called, which served as a detention centre for debtors. The cost to the prisoner for a bed was a shilling a night but some prisoners were charged more. The other prison was Newgate which was sited near the gates of the city near the present Cornmarket. Here likewise, the prisoners were obliged to pay for a bed but if they could not or would not pay the prisoners were beaten and kept in cells or cellars without beds or bedding. Some were kept in chains. The only light in these places were loophole in the walls. It is not surprising that the Channel Row nuns were willing to pay for those priests, Dominican or others known to them who were kept in these conditions when they were arrested.[94] The money paid to the jailers was known as 'garnish money', a term

93. Fagan, *The Second City*, p 23
94. Douglas Bennett, *Encyclopedia of Dublin* (Dublin: Gill & Macmillan) Revised and Expanded edition 2005

borrowed from legal language meaning money to settle a debt or a claim. Vagrants, prostitutes and debtors were held there also:

> [P]risoners were usually required to pay a rent for their accommodation ... In the Black Dog the rent was a shilling per night and those who could not afford to pay were lodged in the dungeons. The gaoler also carried on an extensive trade by selling liquor to the prisoners ... The contribution for ale demanded of each prisoner was known as the Penny-Pot ... If a prisoner could not or would not contribute the required amount, he was likely to find, when he awoke the following morning that his clothing and footwear had disappeared.[95]

Household Expenses

Expenses connected with the running of the convent in Channel Row very often carry the names of those with whom the community dealt. Sometimes personal names are given, sometimes just their trade. 'Mr Kane, the Attorney,' 'Patrick, to making a quilling frame', the smith, the huckster woman, the basket woman, the French man 'for wine'. 'Mr Shaughnessy for copy of a will'; to the goldsmith for a little spoon and 'putting arms on ye little spoon, 9s 6d.' The visit of the Dominican Provincial and the profession days of the nuns were usually celebrated in style and included wine served at dinner. The entry usually read: 'paid for dinner for ye company'. All accounts were dealt with in a very professional manner. Though there was a garden attached to the convent and a gardener was employed, the produce of the garden was not sufficient to supply the needs of such a large household. Some of the garden space would have been given over to walks for the community and boarders.

Channel Row was an enclosed community; the nuns went out only in a hired carriage for business reasons or to go 'to the country' for the good of their health. 'Coach hire, Mrs Burke to buy bed, 2s 2d'.[96] Incidentally, the bed is noted as being for a Miss Falvey and cost £2.10s.0d. There are monthly entries for vegetables, sometimes referred to as 'roots, sellery, turnips, potatoes, greens', all bought from the nearby Ormond Market.

---

95. Fagan, *The Second City*, pp 55-56
96. *Account Book* No 6. See Appendix 3

The woman who did the marketing was paid separately. The
system of purchasing provisions was two-fold. Each month certain basic provisions were contracted for: meat, butter, milk,
eggs, and these were noted separately at the end of the expenditure page. Tea and coffee were sometimes bought but the regular drink was beer. The nuns had their own brew house and they
paid a brewer to process the hops and malt to make the beer.
Repairs to the brew house also feature in the books. All other
purchases are itemised apart from the contracted goods and include everything from nails to mend chairs to the purchase of
beds, payment of rent, taxes, legal fees, travel expenses, doctor,
apothecary, coal man and wages. The nuns used snuff; we know
this from the many entries for it over the years and lest there be
any doubt it is stated 'for the family'. Spitoons were a necessary
if unpleasant adjunct to snuff-taking and they too feature in the
books. The accounting is all-inclusive and meticulously accurate. At times contracts are drawn up for the kind of jobs which
today might not normally require one:

> Memorandum I've agreed with Terence Hynes ye 26 day of
> March 1728 till ye 30 day of June next that he is to keepe ye gar-
> den clean and in good order and always keep salets, roots ...
> [illegible] herbs and every other thing proper for ye kitchen in
> its season as ye ground will afford and he's obliged to spend
> three hole days in ye week during ye time mentioned and if he
> fails in any of yet aforementioned articles he's to forfeit ten
> shillings of his quarters wages which will be twenty shillings a
> quarter and he's to carry all ye rubage out of ye garden and to
> ye garden bring in ye dung at his own cost and that he's to
> serve as ye whole year accordingly if Mrs Browne be satisfied
> as witness my hand this 26 day of March 1728.
> Signed: Terence Hynes.[97]

The contract was fulfilled and as proof the next entry is:

> I acknowledge to have recd from Mrs. Browne the sum of
> one pound for a quarter's wages ending ye 26th day of ye
> month as witness my hand this 25th day of June 1728.
> Signed: Terence Hynes

---

97. *Account Book* No 1

The ladies of Channel Row were women who liked to have their household business conducted in a proper manner as this contract shows. From the context we see that the 'Mrs Browne' who signed the contract was prioress at that time; she is no other than Julia Browne of Brussels fame. The nuns were referred to as 'Mrs' not 'Sister' until well into the eighteenth century, when it was not so necessary for them to keep a low profile.

Nuns, being human, can have disputes and differences of opinion not withstanding their vowed lives. Almost twenty years previously in 1746 there seems to have been some dispute about the allocation of cells to various members of the community:

> We the undersigned sisters of ye Community of ye monastery of Jesus, Mary, Joseph of ye Order of St. Dominick of ye City of Dublin, do now *for peace sake* give Mrs Mary Kelly present prioress ye cell wherein Mrs Mary of ye Holy Ghost Vaughan now lies in, I mean when said Prioress finishes her time, and that said Mrs Vaughan will afterwards lie in ye work house wherein Mrs Taaffe lies, ye workroom that was, to be hereafter ye noviciate and Mrs Sara Kelly to sleep there till there are novices, and afterwards in ye room ye present prioress lies in as witness our hands this 1 day of August 1746.[98]

Not alone did the prioress and eight councillors sign that statement, the Provincial, Michael Hoare, also put his name to it. The dispute about the allocation of the community cells must have been serious indeed to warrant such formality.

Living with the Dominican nuns in the mid-eighteenth century could have been a lively and interesting experience both for the school boarders and parlour boarders who were interested in theatre and music and who had the means of availing of the opportunities which living in the centre of Dublin gave them. Attending the theatre and concerts would be deemed by the nuns to be part of a liberal education suitable for the young ladies in the school.

---

98. *Account Book* No 2 (Italics added)

CHAPTER SEVEN

Community Life
Later years

The day to day life of the Dominicans in Channel Row probably
followed a pattern much as was the custom of all religious of
their time. Early rising at about 5.15 or 5.30 am was followed by
a period of meditation, the recitation of the Divine Office and
Mass, if there was a priest to celebrate it for them. Teaching in
the school and the care of the lady boarders occupied them during the day; they came together in the evening for the Divine
Office and for a period of private prayer and recreation before
retiring for the night. The Galway community rose at midnight
on certain feasts to celebrate the Office of Matins but it is not
known if the Channel Row nuns kept up that tradition; they
probably did so for as long as possible, considering their devotion
to the Divine Office. New convent foundations of all orders in
the eighteenth and nineteenth centuries tended to model their
religious life on the 'mother house'. Channel Row community
was from the beginning an autonomous house but the nuns
would naturally keep the traditional practices of the Galway
convent. The religious habit was not worn for many years after
the nuns came to Dublin. They probably wore something in the
style of the Dominican third order ladies who lived around Co
Mayo and whose dress has already been described.[99] 'They
were referred to as 'Mrs Bellew's family in Channel Row' and
were known to have a 'boarding school for young ladies.' This
disguise was necessary as there had been raids by the authorities on the Poor Clares who lived in the Channel Row convent
prior to the Dominicans. In 1718

the officers sent for three carriages into which were crammed
as many as each would hold together with a bailiff to prevent
their escape. They were conducted to Judge Caulfield's,

99. See Chapter 1 page 18

where to ascertain if they wore no badge of religious profession, they were made to take off their garments and to undergo the most minute investigation as to their manner of life.[100]

The Dominicans were aware of these happenings and had to be circumspect about their dress and anything which might draw the attention of the authorities to their way of life.

There is a description of the Poor Clares' dress at the time, 'a black stuff gown and plain linen', and both communities lived more or less 'as ladies living quietly in the world might do'.[101] The only mention of a religious habit is made on the death of one of the community; the entry in the account books on these occasions reads: 'Payed for White Sarge'. The last raid on the convents reported in a Dublin daily paper, occurred in 1739 when both the Dominicans and Poor Clares were visited by the soldiers: 'Last week upon a false information of arms being lodged in the boarding schools of Channelrow and King's Street, the same was searched but none could be found'.[102]

Liturgical Life

As Dominicans, the Channel Row community was very devoted to the church's liturgy. The Mass and the Divine Office were their principal prayer. In 1725 Stephen Radcliff, the Protestant vicar of Naas, was in controversy with the Reverend Mr Synge, prebendary of St Patrick's Cathedral Dublin. Synge had preached a sermon before the Irish House of Commons in which he recommended the toleration of popery. Radcliff advised Synge that:

> 'no Divine of our Church can be so absurd to Recommend a Toleration of Popery ... and if the Clergy of our Church begin to discover such Inclinations, the Lord have mercy upon us and avert the Evil Day which may come upon this Church and Nation.[103]

Radcliffe's rebuke to Edward Synge was answered by an

100. H. Concannon, *The Poor Clares*, p. 92
101. Ibid, p 96
102. *Dublin Daily Post*, 31 July 1739
103. S. Radcliffe, Pamphlet, *A Letter to the Reverend Mr Edward Synge* (Dublin: 1725)

Portion of Rocque's 1757 Map of Dublin. Channel Row Nunnery is
marked north of Smith Field and Red Cow Lane.

'Julia Browne
Candlestick'
inscribed:
'Pray for Julia
Browne, 1727.'
Browne family
crest etched on
oval cartouche.

Silver Candlesticks on Octagonal bases 1718.
Inscribed: 'Pray for the soul of Mary Bellew, 1721'.

Base of candlestick showing inscription.

Silver Dove Sanctuary Lamp
Inscribed: Channel Row, Dublin 1729
'Lux perpetua luceat eis.'
Another Browne family gift.

Channel Row Convent 1717-1808
Chapel to the left of the main building

Dominican Convent, Vernon Avenue, Clontarf
1808-1819

St Mary's Dominican Convent, Cabra 1819
Sketch of the original house

Reliquary Ebony Cross c.1732,
used during Holy Week ceremonies in Channel Row Convent

anonymous letter defending Synge. Radcliffe published a further pamphlet in which he gave the attendance of some
Protestants at the Mass in Channel Row as proof of a certain
leniency towards the papists:

> You have reason to applaud and celebrate the benign influ-
> ence of the connivance which his late Majesty, his Ministers
> and Magistrates (as you say) were pleased in their goodness
> to afford you ... it may likewise be dangerous ... especially if
> the [present] Government should come to know that under
> the colour of this Pretended Connivance, you have erected
> MONASTERIES and NUNNERIES in several parts of the
> Kingdom and particularly, a Famous convent of the latter in
> Channel Row in Dublin, where the most celebrated Italian
> musicians help to make the voices of the Holy Sisters more
> melodious; and many Protestant Fine Gentlemen have been
> invited to take their places in a convenient gallery, and hear
> the performances.[104]

Two years before Radcliffe's bitter complaints about the
chapel, Dr Stephen MacEgan, a Dominican had been consecrated
Bishop of Clonmacnoise and in the 1730s two other bishops
were consecrated there: a Dominican Bishop Colman O'Shaughnessy of Ossory and Bishop Lawrence Richardson of Kilmore.[105]
There is a traditional belief, not authenticated by any written
evidence, that the first occasion on which the 'Adeste Fideles' was
sung publicly in Dublin, was in the Dominican chapel in
Channel Row.

The adornment of their chapel, its ornaments, sacred vessels
and vestments was important to the nuns. The account books
list in the inventories all the treasures devoted to the worship of
God. Throughout the books there are nine inventories dating
from the first in 1726 to the last in 1768. The most important
pieces mentioned are the large altar-piece painting of the crucifixion which is said to be 'after the manner of Van Dyck' and is
believed to have been given in the time of James II, most likely
through the Earl of Tyrconnell. Julia Browne's family gift of can-

104. S. Radcliffe, *Letter to Synge*; Pamphlet: *A Serious and Humble Enquiry*
(Dublin: 1727) p 69
105. *Cabra Annals* pp 48-49

dlesticks and plate lamp have already been mentioned as has
the Bellew's gifts of church plate and a pipe organ for the
chapel.[106] The Browne candlesticks bear a maker's mark with
the date 1719 and have an oval cartouche with Julia Browne's
name inscribed on it. The plate lamp is a chandelier with eight S-
shaped branches arranged in two tiers of graduated size. There
was also mention of a Holy Week candlestick – a large triangular
candlestick bearing thirteen candles. It was used during the office of Tenebrae, an office of psalms and readings sung in the
evenings of the last three days of Holy Week. The candles were
extinguished one by one during the singing of the psalms; the
candles represented Christ and the Apostles. An ebony plated
cross reliquary dates form 1732 and must be that mentioned annually in the account books: 'Received on the cross on Good
Friday, £2.10.01.' The money was donated by the congregation.[107]
A silver chalice mentioned in 1726 dates from the days of exile
in Spain; it bears no date 'but has been pronounced to be un-
questionably of Spanish make'.[108] Eleven sets of vestments in-
sured that the celebrant was fittingly dressed for all ceremonies.
'One blew set' is thought to have been another link with the
nuns' Spanish and Galway past.

Spirituality
A pointer to the spirituality of the nuns is a list of the books
which formed part of their library. Spirituality refers to any religious or ethical value that is manifested as an attitude of spirit
from which one's actions flow. For a Christian, the only authentic
spirituality is one centred in the person of Jesus Christ and
though him to the Blessed Trinity.[109]

The following are the books listed in the inventories of the
Account Books:

Life of St Teresa	Ye Works of St Teresa
Lives of Ye Saints	Ye Old Testament
Sinner's Guide by Lewis of Grenada	Three tomes of Rodriguez

---

106. See page 57
107. *Account Book* No 4, April 1747; see illustrations following p 64
108. *Cabra Annals*, p 37
109. J. Aumann, *Spiritual Theology* (London: 1980) p 17

Holy Court   Four Meditation Books
Ye Dayle Exercise for Religious   A Practical Catechism
Epistles of Avila [St Teresa]   One Martirologie
Ye Kingdom of God in ye Soull   One Processionary
     Introduction to a Devout Life by St Francis de Sales
     Treatise on the Love of God by St Francis de Sales
     A Book containing ye fruitful sayings of holy David[110]

A liturgical directory or calendar, which was purchased annually, the Processionary and the Martyrology emphasised the
commitment of the community to the Divine Office as their
main prayer. 'Paid for directories for ye quire' is a regular entry
in the *Account Books*, 1717-1817. The Processionary sets out the
rubrics to be observed and the chants sung during ceremonial
processions on feastdays, while the Directory or Ordo is a calendar of feasts of the church and offices to be recited each day of
the liturgical year. At the daily morning office the martyrology
was read outlining very briefly the lives and deaths of the saints.
One would expect to find the scriptures and the lives of the
saints in every monastic and convent library.

     The works of St Teresa of Avila feature in the above list.
Teresa was a sixteenth century reformer and mystic and her
spirituality is akin to that of Dominicans and was much influenced by St.Teresa's Dominican spiritual directors. Her teaching
is found in three major works, *The Life, The Way of Perfection* and
The Interior Castle. Father Aumann, an authority on spirituality
says: 'As a means of growth in holiness she, [Teresa] gives special attention to the reception of communion, the cultivation of
humility, obedience, fraternal charity, the observance of poverty
but above all, the love of God'.[111] Saint Francis de Sales, the
founder and spiritual director of the Visitation nuns of the seventeenth century, was noted for his gentle but firm direction of
the nuns of the Visitation:

     he is regarded as the bridge between the Renaissance and the
     modern period and has been one of the strongest single in-
     fluences on spirituality from the seventeenth century to the
     present day ... From a doctrinal point of view, one of the

110. *Account Book* No 1 1726
111. J. Aumann, *Christian Spirituality in the Catholic Tradition* (London:
1985) p 191

most significant contributions of St Francis de Sales to spiritual theology was to unify all Christian morality and holiness under the bond of charity. This doctrine, to be sure, had been taught explicitly by Saint Thomas Aquinas but by the time of St Francis de Sales it was necessary to insist again that Christian perfection … [consists] in the love of God and neighbour.[112]

The three tomes of Alfonso Rodriguez deal with methods of meditative prayer. The only book listed by a Dominican author is *The Sinner's Guide* which was written by the Provincial of Portugal, Father Lewis of Granada. It treats of the practice of virtue, the redemption, predestination, justification, and the four last things – death, judgement, heaven, hell. Lewis of Granada was renowned in his day for his writings on mystical theology; he was in the mainstream of Catholic spirituality, very orthodox, and his work was a standard authority on spirituality for religious.

Other aspects of the nuns' spirituality are evident from the *Cabra Annals*. There are records of correspondence with Rome, procuring indulgences and spiritual privileges. Theologically an indulgence 'is a divinely recognised remission of temporal punishment for sins whose guilt has already been remitted. It is received when specific conditions are fulfilled by a baptised person: prayer with the reception of the sacraments of Reconciliation and the Eucharist'.[113] Three times in the *Account Books* letters from Rome conveying indulgences are mentioned, in 1728, 1731, and 1739/40. The indulgence granted in 1728 was for visiting the Channel Row chapel and praying 'for concord among Christian Princes, the extirpation of heresy and the Exaltation of Holy Mother Church'.[114]

The devotions recommended for the other indulgences were similar; the days on which the indulgences could be gained were marked as festivals. These were days when the nuns could receive the Eucharist, a privilege much valued by them as fre-

---

112. Ibid, pp 211 and 217
113. C. J. Peter, 'Indulgences' in *The New Dictionary of Theology*, ed J. A. Komonchak, M. Collins, D. A. Lane (Dublin: 1987) pp 513-15.
114. *Cabra Annals*, p 41

quent Communion was not common until the papacy of Pius X in the early twentieth century.

In 1733 the community was granted faculties to erect in their chapel the Confraternity of the Most Holy Rosary, a truly Dominican devotion which combines prayerful meditation on the life and death of Jesus with the recitation of a series of Our Fathers and Hail Marys. Candles were bought each year for the feast of Candlemas in February, another indication of the community's devotion to the liturgy and to the Blessed Virgin Mary. A paschal candle was provided each Easter.

The only record of sermons or instruction from Dominican priests which has survived is given in Hugh Fenning's edition of *The Fotrell Papers*.[115] Fotrell was the Dominican Provincial of Ireland 1738-42. Having carried out a visitation in Channel Row in March 1738, he left written ordinations for the nuns; there are nine altogether. Some deal with the spiritual life of the community, Mass and the reception of the sacraments, 'at least once in 15 days, in Lent and in Advent once in 8 days'. The time of the recital of the office in the morning was laid down: 'in the summer at six and in winter at seven'. Regarding daily living, Father Fotrell prescribed that the 'nuns should not go abroad without urgent need and necessity ... none shall go alone, nor to any place but to such as the superior gives them leave to goe and ... shall not goe otherwise than in a coach they shall be home before night'. The cost of hiring a coach for business is given at fairly frequent intervals. Care of the sick is stressed by Father Fotrell: they should be supplied with all that they need and the community could afford. The list of medicaments which is in *Account Book* No 1 was drawn up in Julia Browne's time as prioress; the list includes mixtures, pills, purging powders, and unguent (ointment). Obviously the injunction to care for the sick was obeyed. Fottrell also ordained uniformity in dress for the community; the use of ruffles, whether at home or abroad was not allowed and 'none ... shall wear or lye in linnen'.[116] Woollen sheets, were *de rigeur* and were reckoned to be more penitential than linen. In 1738/9 a profession ceremony was recorded in

115. H. Fenning, ed. *The Fotrell Papers 1721-39* (PRONI) pp 113-120
116. H. Fennning, *The Fotrell Papers*, pp 106-7

Channel Row at which the provincial preached. The theme of
the sermon was the vows of religious life, the practice of virtue,
the following of Christ. The Blessed Virgin Mary was to be held
in veneration as a model for religious. Another short sermon
given to the nuns after visitation exhorts them to practice charity
among themselves and to be exact in the fulfilment of their religious duties.

Canonical visitations, retreats and sermons on the practice of
charity and adherence to the rule and constitutions are necessary and useful reminders to religious of a commitment given at
the time of profession. Apart from occasions such as the profession of a new member, retreats and visitations, the election of
the prioress was always presided over by the Provincial of the
Irish Province and was followed by a festive meal with 'a bottle
of wine for the Provincial's visit' duly noted in the *Account
Books*. In the end papers inside the covers of some of the *Account
Books* there are notes about community affairs not directly connected with finance and which today would be kept in special
registers of elections or in the community annals. An example of
this is seen in the following note of the election of the prioress
Mary Kelly in 1765:

> This twentieth day of Augt 1765 the Reverend Mother Mary
> Kelly was confirmed Prioress of Channelrow at half an hour
> and ten minits after two of the clock on Tuesday.[117]

---

117. *Account Book* No 6

CHAPTER EIGHT

Schooling for Catholics
in eighteenth-century Ireland

The popular conception of Catholic education in the eighteenth century in Ireland is that of a people totally deprived of schooling. The 1695 legislation and those of the 1700s (the Penal Laws) prohibited Catholics who could afford to do so from sending their children abroad to receive a Catholic education. The Acts also forbade anyone to tutor a Catholic family or teach in a Catholic school. There were colleges on the continent in France, Belgium and Spain, which prepared young men for the priesthood. Over the course of the century many were smuggled out of the country and returned as ordained priests or if they did not become ordained priests, some returned as educated people. For Catholics in general, therefore, there was no higher education available in the country and according to law no education at any level should be provided for them. The intention of the government was that the Catholic population should be kept in a position of inferiority, socially and economically. The laws were successful to a large degree but, as Corish says, 'it is not historical to see the penal laws as having reduced all Catholics to the same level of deprivation'.[118]

The enactment of law and its implementation or enforcement are two separate realities. To assess the risk taken by Mary Bellew and her community in operating a boarding school for girls in Channel Row, one must consider how in fact the laws were enforced at any given time. There was a variation in the harassment of Catholics according to the political climate over the course of the eighteenth century. The penal code of 1691 forbade 'papists to teach school publicly or in private houses, except to children of the family'.[119] In 1703 in the reign of Queen

118. P. Corish, *The Catholic Community in the Seventeenth and Eighteenth Centuries* (Dublin: 1981) p 82
119. M. Ronan, 'Catholic Schools of Old Dublin', in *Dublin Historical Record*, Vol XII, No 3 pp 65-82

Anne another act of parliament was passed adding to the severity of the punishment meted out to any 'popish regular clergy-
man' who disobeyed the law. Such a person would, on first con-
viction, incur all the penalties and forfeitures and would be
liable to prison transportation to the tobacco and cotton plant-
ations owned by English interests in America. On second con-
viction he would be condemned to death for high treason.
Catholics were asked to swear that Anne was the rightful queen
and that the Stuart claimant had no right to the crown. This pro-
cedure was called the oath of abjuration and it also had a clause
in the formula denying the Mass.[120] In 1765 there was a convic-
tion of a 'popish schoolmaster', Charles Grey, for keeping 'a
popish school'. Grey was fined £20 and was imprisoned for
three months. He was unable to pay the fine and had it reduced
to 6d (sixpence) 'by reason of his great poverty'. He had to give
assurances of his good behaviour and 'not commit a like offence
in the future'. The state hoped that by strictly implementing
these penalties 'popish children might by resorting to English
schools (i.e. in Ireland) and learning the English tongue, be
brought to see the error and blindness of their predecessors.'[121]
In that way the state hoped popish schools could be suppressed
altogether. Charity schools were set up in 1712 by a memorial of
James Duke of Ormond, the Viceroy; the object of the schools
was stated openly to be: 'That the whole nation may in time be
made both Protestant and English.'[122] Dean Swift carried out
this plan in that same year, 1712, and opened two charity
schools in St Patrick's in the Liberties in Dublin. This was the
year of the arrival of the Poor Clare nuns in Dublin from Galway
and they were installed in Channel Row to be followed five
years later by the Dominicans led by Mary Bellew.[123]

Hedge Schools
In spite of these laws and prohibitions there were those who
flouted the law and taught small numbers of pupils throughout

120. 1709, 8 Queen Anne C.3
121. M. Ronan, 'Catholic Schools of Old Dublin', p 74
122. Ibid, p 75
123. See chapter 11 for further information about the Poor Clares in
Ireland

the country. The fame of the hedge schools was widespread. The image of the poor badly-dressed man sheltering under a hedge, teaching a small number of children is familiar to Irish people; many who flouted the law paid for their temerity. Sometimes the schoolmaster was allowed to take his class in an outhouse or in some sheltered place. Oral and written history records many of these hedge school masters, sometimes staying in a locality and if they had cause to fear capture and arrest, they moved on to a safer place. They were sometimes given board and lodgings by the poor people who valued an education for their children and who willingly paid a small fee of a few pence per week. John Howard FRS, a noted philanthropist, observed in 1782:

At the cabins on the roadside I saw several schools in which for the payment of 3s.3d Irish per quarter, children were instructed in reading, writing and accounts. Some of these I examined as to their proficiency and found them much forwarder than those of the same age in the Charter Schools. They were clean and wholesome.[124]

Some of these teachers would have belonged to the group already mentioned who had been educated on the continent but had not been ordained priests. They had a good grounding in the classics and they passed on that knowledge to their pupils. Irish literature is rich in references to seemingly uneducated people quoting Greek and Latin classical authors, much to the surprise of travellers to Ireland. Irish poetry is strewn with allusions to classical mythology, sometimes using them as metaphors for the Stuarts and expressing a longing for their return. Vision songs (*aislingí*) were a favourite device of poets at the time. The poet dreams of a beautiful lady, Ireland in disguise, who appears and promises the return of the Stuarts. In *Úr-Chill an Chreagáin*, Art Mac Cumhaigh, an Ulster poet 1723-1773, questions the 'vision'. In the style of the time he uses some of these classical references:

A ríoghain dheas mhilis, an tú Helen fár tréaghadh sló,
Nó an de naoi mná deasa thú ó Pharnassus bhí déanta i gcló,

124. T. Corcoran, 'Popular education in the Ireland of 1825', in *Studies*, Vol XIV (Dublin: March 1925) p 42

Goidé tír insa chruinne dár hoileadh thú, a réalt gan cheo.
Ler mhian leat mo shamhailse bheith ag cognarnaigh leat siar sa ród?

O pleasant sweet princess, are you Helen caused ruin to '
hordes?
Or one of the nine from Parnassus so shapely in form?
Or where in the world were you reared, unclouded star
That you want to go whispering West with my likes on the
road?[125]

Town Schools
While this covert educational system was in place in some parts
of the country, there was also a more formal type of schooling
being provided in other places, especially in the towns. The laws
existed on the statute books but enforcement was not always
carried out, especially when the threat of foreign invasion had
receded; this support would have been given by Stuart supporters from Europe, especially from France or Spain. As the country settled down under the Hanoverians, that is the Georges,
those who conducted schools were not disturbed very often.
Even Mass houses were allowed to exist and Mass was celebrated
openly. In the archdiocese of Dublin there were, 'apart from
chapels in the city and its "liberties", fifty-eight Mass houses, of
which twenty-four had been built since 1714'.[126]

Toleration as distinct from encouragement was given to
those who set up schools and teachers gained courage to take
chances as time passed. In an official Report on Popery commis-
sioned by the Irish House of Lords 1731, it was stated that in the
parish of St Michan's alone, there were nine schools, two Latin
schools and seven English schools. All of these were run by
Catholic schoolmasters. The Latin or classical schools taught
boys with a view to their going to a college on the continent for
further education, usually for the priesthood, or for medical
studies, one of the few professions open to Catholics. Many of
the schools were 'pay schools' for the education of the better off

125. S. Ó Tuama and T. Kinsella, eds., *An Duanaire, Poems of the Dispossessed*, (Mountrath: 1981) pp 178, 179.
126. L. M. Cullen, *Life in Ireland in the Eighteenth Century* (London: 1968)
pp 95, 96

and the number of pupils was very limited. As few as ten or fifteen children attended each one. The most famous of these
schools in its day was Fr Austin's Classical Academy; Father
Austin was a Jesuit and for a time his school served as a semin-
ary for the diocese of Meath in the latter part of the eighteenth
century. In Dublin there were not many opportunities for education for girls; the difficulties of sustaining schools tended to
concentrate the attention of concerned people on boys' education.
In some parishes women did teach girls; this was the only hope
they had of getting an elementary education but many children
got none.[127] Whyte's School and the Hibernia Society School
catered for girls, but only for Protestants. In 1731 the Lords'
Report said that there were five 'popish schools' all taught by
lay women and sixteen 'popish schoolmasters some of whom
were priests or friars'. The women's schools were: 'Mill Street,
New Roe, Combe, Truck Street, and St Nicholas Without the
Walls.' The Report went on the say that in the parish of St Paul,
'a nunnery in Channel Row commonly goes under the name of a
boarding school.'[128] In 1733 the Charter Schools were set up to
provide an education 'where the children of poor Catholics
would receive an industrial education and be brought up in the
Protestant faith.'[129] The proselytising nature of the Charter
schools worked against their success; Catholics were suspicious
of them and many did not willingly send their children to these
schools.

Channel Row Boarding School
It was against this political and social background that Mary
Bellew opened the boarding school in Channel Row; it was one
of the first to open its doors to Catholic girls and continue until
the 1760s. We have no documentary evidence to tell us what the
nuns' thoughts were on educational matters or how they felt
about the lack of educational facilities for the children of the
poor who lived in their locality. In the 1750s, reporting to Rome
on abuses by the friars in Ireland, the Dominican nuns in
Channel Row were criticised by a Canon Murphy for not taking

127. R. Burke Savage, *A Valiant Woman* (Dublin :1940) pp 43-48
128. Ronan, 'Catholic Schools in Old Dublin' p 65-82
129. Beckett, *The Making of Modern Ireland*, p 182

more interest in teaching the poor. Incidentally he also stressed their lack of formal cloister, their wearing lay clothes, and the scandal they gave by frequently going out of their convent.[130] They were women of their time and class and may not have given the subject of the education of poor girls any thought. They had originally come from Galway where there had been a boarding school under the care of their community. Their predecessors had been in exile in Spain where they too had experience of teaching in a boarding school for the better-off members of society. It may have been part of their thinking in coming to Dublin that their main means of livelihood would be a school where they were sure of the patronage of their families.

Not until the end of the century did Nano Nagle (1728-84) in Cork and Teresa Mulally (1728-1803) in George's Hill Dublin begin their work for the free education of poor girls. Edmund Ignatius Rice, founder of the Christian Brothers, did not open a school for poor boys in Hanover Street in Dublin until 1812 though he had schools in other parts of the country prior to that date.[131] Canon Murphy in the 1750s was ahead of the nuns in his thinking about the need for schools for the poor. Teresa Mulally, like the Channel Row nuns earlier in the century, received financial help for her poor school in George's Hill from among others, the Bellews of Barmeath and from other families of Anglo-Norman origin.[132] According to Teresa Mulally's biographer, Teresa had considered entering religious life either with the Dominicans in Channel Row or the Poor Clares in King Street but Teresa knew the nuns in Channel Row personally and realised that her own commitment lay with the poor among whom she lived and for whom she opened her school in George's Hill.[133]

The Dominican nuns were determined to open a school in spite of the penalties which might follow if they infringed the

130. H. Fenning, *The Irish Dominicans*, p 224
131. Kealy, M., *Dominican Education in Ireland 1820-1930* (Dublin: Irish Academic Press 2007) p 65
132. Archives of Presentation Convent, George's Hill, Dublin, FD 98: 'The Correspondence of Teresa Mulally, 1786'
133. R. Burke Savage, *A Valiant Dublin Woman* (Dublin: Gill & Son, 1940) p 54

penal laws against Catholic education. The convent school 'for young ladies' opened in October 1719 with four pupils: 'Miss Brown, Miss Murphy, Miss Corcoran and Miss Geoghegan.'[134] The fee was £12 per annum payable in installments of £4 a quarter. The numbers increased each month for a time until it reached an average of about twenty pupils. Some remained in the school for short periods only, sometimes for two or three quarters; others stayed a year or two. There are no accurate yearly numbers recorded. The education the girls received was that deemed suitable for young ladies of their social status who would take their places afterwards as cultured and accomplished women. Their role in society would be as wives and mothers unless they opted for religious life. Some made that choice; at least twenty-four entered over the hundred years, 1719-1819. A list of names of those who were pupils in 1725 shows that many of them were of the same social background as the nuns:

> two Burkes, daughters of Lord Mayo
> two Nugents, daughters of Lord Riverston of Westmeath
> one Browne, a daughter of Lord Kenmare
> two Plunketts, daughters of Lord Dunsany
> two Barnwalls, daughters of Lord Trimleston
> a daughter of Lady Cavan
> a daughter of Lady Rice
> two daughters of Viscount Netterville.[135]

The regime in the school was probably quietly ordered. Great emphasis was laid on a good grounding in religious education, English, French, Music, and Drawing. Dancing was an optional extra: 'Payed Miss Molly Reily's Dancing Master, 9s.5d'. An item, 'Payed for fiddle-strings' appears quite often in the *Account Books* so the violin at least was taught and evidently vigorously practised. The records have just one list of school books dating from about 1812 and used when the school had moved to Clontarf. It is possible that the curriculum had not changed much from the days of the Channel Row school. There was an emphasis on French language teaching: a French grammar,

134. *Cabra Annals*, p 32 and *Account Book* No 1
135. Cabra Archives, *Account Book* No 1

Fontaine's *Fables* and Chombaud's *Fables* are the only books apart from history and geography texts mentioned. Nothing can be deduced from this list except that it is a very short one and probably does not reflect the full curriculum taught. Lay teachers were employed; there is mention of a 'Writing Master', two governesses, Miss Walshe and Miss Hughes, and another reference to engaging 'Mr Farrell, to teach Writing, Accounts, Arithmetic, Geography and the use of the Globes at 1 guinea a quarter each lady.'[136] Though written for the Cabra boarding school in 1836 the following excerpt may broadly reflect the ethos of the school in the late 1700s:

> Young ladies are taught in this Establishment the usual branches of English Education, Italian, French, Music, and Needlework plain and ornamental for the sum of £25 per ann … Dancing £2 per session. No vacation will be allowed. The Nuns solely intent on being usefully employed in promoting the temporal and eternal welfare of their Pupils, will not in any manner sanction the imprudence of Parents, who, attaching undue importance to what is called a fashionable education, waste time and money in having their Children taught, to the exclusion of useful and necessary knowledge, accomplishments for which they have neither taste, capacity nor use.[137]

The nuns made it clear that the social position of the pupils was important and that in educating them they would ensure that the girls were made aware of that position:

> no effort shall be left untried to make them so acquainted with the nature and fitness of things, that should circumstances permit them fairly to rise in society, they will naturally take their own places and fill them with propriety, ease and dignity.[138]

When the school was thriving in the mid 1740s and 1750s it was not uncommon for the 'Boarding School in Channel Row' to merit a mention in the Dublin newspapers; unfortunately the items were all of a melancholy nature:

136. *Cabra Annals*, p 73
137. *Complete Catholic Directory and Almanack 1836* (Dublin: 1836) p 162
138. *Complete Catholic Directory and Almanack 1836*, p 163

Saturday, a young lady at the Boarding School in Channel Row died suddenly as she was at dinner.

On Thursday night some villains broke into the Nunnery in Channel Row and carry'd off several valuable goods belonging to the young ladies who board there.

Saturday night, died at the Boarding School in Channel Row Miss Jane Bodkin, a young lady of very good character.[139]

Jane Bodkin was a young member of the community at the time of her death.

There is no record of how the past pupils fared in their later years except for those who joined the community. The overall number of nuns for the period 1717-1819 was fifty-three. When they were flourishing in the mid-century, the maximum number in community at any one time was twenty-seven nuns. There are two official lists naming the members, one list is given by de Burgo in 1756 and the other list is for 1767, drawn up by Fr Netterville, the Irish Provincial of the time.[140] In the same report the Provincial writes tersely: *'Notandum quod S. Anna Blake ab hoc monasterium aufugit ab octo circa annis, et ubinam sit nescimus'* – Sr Anna Blake fled this monastery about eight years ago, we do not know to where.'[141] Sr Anna Blake's name is in the 1756 list, her age at that time is given as twenty and she was one year professed. This fleeing must have caused grief and upset to the community; the use of the word *'aufugit'* has overtones of surprise and consternation. The rider, 'we do not know to where' adds to the sense of bewilderment. Oral tradition alleges that she eloped with the apothecary. Anna must have realised after her profession that life in the convent was not for her. In the meantime, in another part of the building or perhaps in one or more of the houses acquired by the community alongside the convent in Channel Row, the parlour boarders enjoyed their life as part of the community or at least living a comfortable, tranquil life in surroundings which if not luxurious, then at least in modest comfort and security.

---

139. *Pue's Occurrences*, September 1743 and October 1754; *Dublin Intelligence*, May 1730

140. De Burgo, *Hibernia Dominicana*, p 360; Unpublished *Report of Provincial of Ireland to Master of the Order* Archives of Dominican Order (1767)

141. Ibid, the pages of the handwritten transcript of the Report of Provincial are not numbered

80

CHAPTER NINE

Parlour Boarders and Bank Bonds

The most distinguished parlour boarders of Channel Row were Lady Tyrconnell and her daughters who head the long list of titled ladies, at least ten are named, who stayed in the convent at various times paying pensions for 'dyet and lodgings'. The names of others also feature, suggesting that they came from middle class families as distinct from the gentry: O'Neill, Egan, Welsh, Daly, Quigly, are names taken at random from the *Account Books*. Some of the ladies occupied a suite of rooms and had a servant or two: 'Lady Mountgarret's parlour … Miss Coughlan's parlour and bedchamber'.[142] The pension was £16 usually paid half-yearly. In some cases there evidently was a reduction in fees; a certain Mrs Grace paid monthly but the sums paid were not consistently the same. Her account recorded sums between £0.10s.3d to £2.2s.9d. Sometimes a rise in pension is noted: in the April 1745 accounts Mrs Quigly is credited with a quarter's pension of £7.10s.0d 'for her and Mrs Ann' (presumably a relative of Mrs Quigly). In July following, the entry reads: 'Recd from Mrs Quigly a quarter's pension for her and Mrs Ann ending the 13th of this July and raise of pension £8.15s 0d'. Names of mothers and daughters appear in the books: the daughters were school boarders, for example, 'from Mrs Donelan in part of quarter's pension for herself, children and sarvant and raise of pension £20'. Other items of expenditure for the parlour boarders occur: furniture for their rooms, repairs carried out, or the white-washing of walls.

We have no evidence of how these ladies spent their time. Visiting friends and returning calls was fashionable at the time and those ladies who had a 'parlour' had the space and privacy necessary to entertain some of their friends to afternoon tea. Mrs Delany of Delville was a friend of Dean Swift and mentions

142. Cabra Archives, Channel Row collection, *Account Book* No 5

visiting the Poor Clares in King Street for afternoon tea. The
Dominicans and their lady boarders undoubtedly also entertained guests.[143] The Delany house, Delville, was on the site of
the present Bon Secours Hospital in Glasnevin and Mrs Delany
was a well-known society lady at the time. Perhaps the parlour
boarders might have attended some of the social events in the
city; Dublin was renowned for its music and theatre in the eighteenth century. The first public performance of Handel's *Messiah*
ever given, was in the Musick Hall in Fishamble Street, Dublin
in 1742. Fishamble Street is a short distance across the River
Liffey from Channel Row. Perhaps some of the ladies of Channel
Row may have been among those who had been requested not
to wear their hoops to the performance as space in the Musick
Hall was limited.[144] Music and the theatre were the main
sources of entertainment for the middle and upper classes. The
theatres in Smock Alley and Crow Street were also in the vicinity
of Channel Row. Plays and concerts which were popular in
England often were brought to Dublin where there was an ap-
preciative theatre-going public. The music of the baroque com-
posers of the Italian school was much in vogue. (Remember Mr
Radcliffe's annoyance at the nuns having Italian musicians at
the Masses in their chapel.) The works of Handel, Corelli, and
Vivaldi were popular; it is recorded that it cost 'a British Crown'
for admission to a performance of an oratorio'.[145] An entry in the
Channel Row *Account Books*, 'paid, £0.02.08d' to City Musick', a
band sponsored by Dublin Corporation, would lead one to be-
lieve that the band presumably entertained the residents of
Channel Row convent and were paid for their services, or perhaps the money was given as a donation for the upkeep of the
band.

Banking Crises and Bad Debts
In 1756 the boarding school seems to have been at its peak point.
The *Account Books* of later years are not as comprehensive in
their entries as in the earlier years. In 1756 there were twenty-

143. C. Maxwell, *Ireland Under the Georges* (London: 1938)
144. O'Donnell, *The Annals of Dublin*, p 106
145. B. Boydell, *Dublin Musical Calendar 1700-1768* (Dublin: 1988) p 11
and following

seven nuns in the community and eighteen boarders. Numbers of pupils decreased after that and by 1767 there were only three boarders on the roll. The bell was tolling for the Dominicans in Channel Row and the community must have been aware of it but they still had the will to continue. The fall in the financial assets of the Dominican community after the year 1756 is not easy to explain; more evidence is needed of how the nuns used the bonds which were a source of security to them in their lives prior to the mid 1750s. The *Account Books*, our only source, do not give us any detailed information of this kind. L. M. Cullen, in a paper read to the Royal Historical Society on eighteenth-century Irish economic history, says that the Irish banking crises 'are closely tied up with the intermittent commercial crises' and that there were eight banking crises between the 1720s and 1778.[146] Certainly the family fortunes of the nuns' relatives on which they depended so much, seem to have declined after 1756; the numbers in the boarding school fell from eighteen to three, the number of parlour boarders fell from twenty-one and their servants, from six to zero while the bonds' income fell from £6250 in 1756 to £3,600 in 1767. That was a sharp decline indeed and things did not improve for the nuns for many years to come. In the absence of a modern banking system as known to us in the twenty-first century, we do get some idea from the *Account Books* of how the finances were managed or perhaps at times mis-managed. It seems that the community and their clients and friends had a private arrangement of giving and receiving, lending and borrowing, which seems to have been quite complicated. At times, there are two or three parties mentioned in the *Account Books* associated with the bonds and the interest paid, or in some cases not paid; it is difficult to separate the lenders from the borrowers and it is not possible to analyse fully the exchange of bonds between the nuns and their families.

> Bank failures in 1759 (two banks failed in Dublin) made financial houses and the public alike wary of notes payable to bearer. But without issuing notes payable to bearer there

146.L. M. Cullen, 'Problems in the Interpretation and Revision of Eighteenth-century Irish Economic History' in *Transactions of the Royal Historical Society* (Dublin: January 1966)

were many merchants with whom private individuals lodged money and who performed the vital banking functions of providing short-term credit and remitting money around which the whole economic life of the country revolved.[147]

In a small way it would appear that the Channel Row nuns became part of that system, facilitating their families and friends at this time. Most of these families were dependent on land for their income. Bad harvests in 1744, 1752 and 1753 depressed their incomes and grain was imported. Between 1770 and 1771 many merchants were declared bankrupt. The effect of the slump in the markets seeped down through the whole economy. Though the linen trade was fairly stable, the bad harvests affected it also; flax harvests were damaged in the bad weather and the credit crises of 1759, 1760 and 1777 were blamed on these events. The American War of Independence 1775-83 caused a depression in England and a reduction in credit made it difficult for buyers to purchase cattle; prices fell at the fairs. The difficult situation was reflected in the fall of rents; the gentry would have suffered from this fall, as many of them had land rented out to small farmers and cottiers and arrears mounted, leaving the land-owners short of cash.

Returning to our primary source, the *Account Books*, we find that the actual paper bonds were held in the convent in the 'depositum' or convent safe. Recently a box marked 'bonds' was found in the Cabra archives with part of a damaged original eighteenth-century bond in it. The interest on these bonds was used by the community for day-to-day expenses. Eventually it seems that a development of that system evolved whereby the bonds themselves were used by the nuns to pay their debts. In 1756 this entry was made:

> This day it was agreed in Counsell and community that a hundred pound of our ffunds which belongs to Sisr. Sally Dillon shu'd be borrowed to pay Debts and a hundred pounds intrest that is due on Mr. Bodkin's bond to be paid in the place of it, witness our hand ye 25th day of October 1756.[148]

147. L. M .Cullen, *An Economic History of Ireland Since 1660* (London: 1972) p 72
148. *Account Book* No 5. Spelling as in the original

Sally Dillon's dowry money (or part of it) was paid out to cover a debt, and the interest due on another bond was used to repay Sally Dillon. On other occasions the bonds were lent out to third parties. Lady Mountgarret was a parlour boarder in 1756; she got into debt and must have approached the nuns for a loan:

> It is agreed by ye counsel and community ye 27th August 1756 that Lady Mountgarret shall have ye sum of 300 pounds two of wch belongs to Sisr Mary Nugent and one hundred to Sisr Sara Dillon for wch she is to give her bond and warrant joined with her Bror in law Mr Corr and for farther security she gives us a Bill of seal of all her furniture and plate and household goods witness our hand ye above date.
> Signed: Eliza Bourke, Rosa Farrell, Mary Daly.[149]

That loan was well secured not only by Lady Mountgarret's brother-in-law but also by the bill of sale of all her furniture. The furniture was on the premises as part of Lady Mountgarret's suite in the convent.

In the Cabra archives there is a copy of a legal document relating to the O'Gara family. This copy was given to the archivist by a member of the extended family; the details which follow are based on that document. Evidently there was a formal enquiry as to the suitability of a member of the O'Gara family for some unnamed post or, more probably, a church appointment. The person who gave the evidence was

> the Reverend Father Friar Domingo O'Conor of the Order of St Dominic, Provincial Vicar and Solicitor General for the Province of Ireland at this court and finding him in the monastery of La Pasion, we gave him an oath which he took in the *verbo sacerdotis* form.

There is no indication in the pages in the archives of where exactly this hearing took place but is seems to have been in Spain. Mrs O'Gara, whose maiden name was Maria Fleming was born in Slane, Co Meath, and married a Colonel O'Gara from Coolavin, Co Roscommon. The colonel had served in King James' army and accompanied the King 'Jacobo II' in 1692 when

---

149. Ibid

they fled after the Battle of the Boyne. They left 'with many other
noble and loyal families of Ireland' and settled in Spain. The
colonel lost not only his post but 'his own estates and goods
which were confiscated by the heretics'. Mrs O'Gara returned to
Ireland presumably after her husband's death, and 'resigned
herself to dying in a religious Dominican Convent in the city of
Dublin, by the name of the School of Catholic Women.'[150] This
lady, Dona Maria O'Gara, was a parlour boarder in Channel
Row in the 1720s and is recorded as having the following pieces
of furniture in her rooms: To give the reader some idea of the
style of furniture these ladies had, the following list is copied
from the *Account Book* No 1:

One red canopy bed	One eassy chair	One Dressing Glass
One walnut buroe	One foulding Screen	One Grate Fender & Irons
Two oak tables	Two rough chairs	One Close Stool
One Brass Snuffers	One Hearth Bough	Two paper Pictures
One pr. of Glass Branches		One pr. of Brass Candlesticks[151]

The regulations of canon law regarding nuns' dowries were
evidently not as stringent in the eighteenth century as they are
today. The capital sum or principal of a nun's dowry, if she has
such today, may not be spent in the nun's life-time but the interest earned on it during her lifetime may be used for current expenses. In Channel Row when finances were scarce, on at least
one occasion, the principal was used and that on the very day of
a Sister's profession;

> This day Sister Nancy Blake was put to votes for Profession
> and unanimously received by votes, by counsel and commu-
> nity, her fund is 200 pounds wch is to be set out to interest –
> forty pounds besides she gives towards paying Mr Val Egan
> for our Building. As witness our hand this 6th day of Decbr
> 1755. Eliza Bourke.

> This day it is agreed by counsel and community that
> Counseler Costelo shuld have Miss Blake's 200 pounds wch
> is given him and he past his bond & warrant to Mrs Eliza

150. Cabra Archives, O'Gara document (undated)
151. *Account Book* No 1

Bourke and for ye same this 11th day of Decr 1755 ye same night Miss Blake is professed.[152]

This is the same Anna Blake who later fled the monastery.

It is possible to chart the decline of the Channel Row community by comparing the numbers in the community, in the boarding school and the parlour boarders in certain years. Putting the value of the bonds held by the community alongside that information, it is easy to see how they came to be in such a sorry state at the end of the century. The table below sets out those figures. The years are not chosen arbitrarily; 1729 was a year when the nuns were well established in Dublin; in 1744 the number in the school was down to nine. 1756 and 1767 were years in which there are accurate figures for the number of nuns in the community and in 1792 it would seem that things had gone beyond recovery. The community was experiencing great difficulties, their financial state was grave and their numbers were falling fast.

COMPARATIVE TABLE

YEAR	NUNS	BOARDERS	PARLOUR BOARDERS	BONDS' INCOME
1729	22	20	10 + Servants	£5080
1744	16	9	12	£3400
1756	27	18	21 + servants	£6250
1767	19/20	3	6	£3600
1792	5	0	not known	* £1800 [good] £1100 [bad]

NOTE: The Account Books from the 1760s onwards are not as Comprehensive in their entries as the earlier books.

• good = money in hand
bad = money owed to nuns but the recovery of debt doubtful

For list of nuns of Channel Row Convent 1719–1820 see Appendix pp 103-104.

---

152. *Account Book* No 5

CHAPTER TEN

Channel Row – Clontarf – Cabra

About the year 1787-88 a young lady entered the Dominican convent in Channel Row who was to be responsible for that community's revival and survival into the nineteenth century and beyond. Eliza Byrne was a merchant's daughter who had been a parlour boarder in Channel Row before she entered religious life as one of the community. She was professed in Channel Row in 1790 and elected prioress in 1798. She had arrived on the scene when there were very few left in the community, when finances were very low and before the nuns had begun to use the banks for their business affairs. The first mention of a bank in the modern sense does not occur in the Channel Row *Account Books* until 1811, three years after the community left Channel Row and had moved to Clontarf. By that time the nuns were investing in debentures: 'April 1811, from La Touche's Bank, 6 months interest on 14 debentures due £42'. They had then also invested in the Grand Canal Company: '14 debentures bearing 6%'.[153] Eliza Byrne's brother was a business man and gave advice and support to Eliza. It was probably he who advised the small group of three about their finances and its prudent administration.

F. S. L. Lyons in his *Bank of Ireland Bicentenary Essays*, writes of the collapse of the banks in eighteenth century:

> In the first quarter of the eighteenth century there were only a few banks in Ireland and the second half of the century saw the collapse of most of the Irish private banks leaving eventually only four or five in Dublin of which the most prestigious and prominent was La Touche's. It was the only one to last another century.[154]

153. *Account Book* No 8
154. F. S. L. Lyons, ed, *Bicentenary Essays, Bank of Ireland 1783-1983* (Dublin: 1983) p 17

The exchange of bonds which had been the mainstay of the Channel Row community's funds, trickled to a standstill from the 1770s onwards. Bad debts accumulated and the nuns themselves were growing old, few in number, disheartened and they had given up the rental of one of the houses. This is precisely the time when Eliza Byrne became prioress in 1798 and lawsuits which had begun in 1780, went against the community. The financial statement for the year 1801 shows how their fortunes had changed:

Funds and bonds £2,900
Due to the house £1,836.15s.03d
Due by the house £195.17.07d[155]

The lawsuits arose from an attempt to recover some of the money owed to the community:

Thomas N. of Longford Street undertook to receive the following bonds – debts ... Totaling £1,400 .... The bill of attending above Lawsuits amounted to upwards of £900. Thomas N. acknowledged to have received in the business £700. He paid over to the ladies of that money something more than £70. In other business after putting them to vast expense he effected nothing. He got or obtained judgement by default, against them for the remainder of his bill .... The costs in all £838.09s. 00d.[156]

This bill for £838.09.00d seems outrageously excessive in 1798 financial terms. One wonders about the credentials of Thomas N. of Longford Street. He certainly was not a good adviser to the nuns at that time.

When the lease of the Channel Row house expired in 1808 the landlord would not renew it. A factor in his refusal may have been that the House of Industry, (the Poor House) which was situated also in Channel Row was overcrowded and it was known that the authorities were looking for new premises. As some sick people were treated in the House of Industry it was decided to found a new hospital. The convent in Channel Row was nearby and as the lease had run out perhaps the landlord

155. *Cabra Annals* p 70
156. *Account Book* No 8

saw an opportunity to sell it and make a profit on the transaction. Whatever the motivation, the ending of the lease was a lucky strike for the landlord:

> it happened that 'a spacious and commodious building immediately adjoining the grounds of the House of Industry built for a Nunnery,' had a few months ago been vacated by its former inhabitants and was to be disposed of. This house might be rented by the governors and £1,000 be spent on its renovation and maintenance and it could be used by 'the more decent poor.'[157]

A New Century, A New Beginning

The nuns must not have anticipated the ending of the lease on the convent because some time previously they had expended £120 on repairs to the chapel roof. From 1792-96 there were only two names given as councillors, Bell Kirwan, the prioress, and Eliza Byrne. Bell Kirwan had been an invalid for many years and Eliza Byrne in fact conducted the business of the convent. Bell Kirwan died in 1798. Eliza Byrne then became *de facto* the prioress and with her two companions, Lydia Wall and Bridget Strong, Eliza was left to make the preparations to vacate Channel Row and rent a house in Clontarf for 'a fine of £600 and a yearly rental of £100'. The *Cabra Annals* state: 'in all probability there was no one to relieve her of her position'.[158] Eliza Byrne, Lydia Wall and Brigid Strong left Channel Row in the spring of 1808. That is a stark short sentence but the leaving of Channel Row must have been a big upheaval for the three nuns. Some of the parlour boarders went with them but the *Account Books* noted that many had left the house in the previous January and February. The three women were making a new beginning in a house on Vernon Avenue which became known as 'Convent House', a large house with a garden attached. The nuns took two fields from a Mr Fisher, at a yearly rent of £28.8s.8d. During the months of January to March 1808 the furniture was removed from Channel Row to the new convent. It was a costly exercise

157. J. D. H. Widdess, *The Richmond, Whitworth and Hardwick Hospitals, Dublin* (Dublin: 1872) pp 33, 34
158. *Cabra Annals* p 68

for the nuns who now had very little ready cash or investments. Before leaving Channel Row they tried to make money by the sale of some of their unwanted goods: 'received for old furniture sold on leaving Brunswick Street £14.10s.9d.'[159] This was the first time the nuns used the name Brunswick Street in their books though the street name had been changed officially in 1766. From 1717, the year Mary Bellew and her group came from Galway, their successors in the Dominican convent Channel Row lived their religious lives faithfully and conducted the boarding school but in 1808, through misfortune, the three surviving Sisters were forced to move on from a much loved and familiar place and bravely make another start. Using the Brunswick Street name then, may have been a cutting off gesture, unconsciously and psychologically, from their beloved Channel Row.

Clontarf
In Vernon Avenue, Clontarf, the three survivors of Channel Row, Eliza, Lydia and Bridget were determined to make a fresh start and they made the most of their surroundings. They had a good-sized garden together with the fields purchased when they took over the house. They made some money by selling vegetables to the neighbours and letting out the fields. The *Account Books* entries noted: 'received for vegetables', 'for grazing', 'for sheep sold in Smithfield'. They still had the few parlour boarders who came with them from Channel Row and they opened a day school and a small boarding school in August 1808, just six months after their arrival. In some cases they got fees in advance which must have been a help to them: 'Received from Mathew Butler, Esq entrance money, diet and lodging and tuition for his two daughters in advance for six months'.[160] The young ladies who were on roll in the school in the first years were: the Misses Butler, Gerrard, Higgins, Kelly, Loughlin, Mary Kelly, Maria Dillon, Miss Devine, Miss Garrigan, Misses Plunkett, Miss O'Reilly, Miss Mathews, and Miss Alcorn. There are a few familiar surnames among them – Dillon, Plunkett,

---

159. *Cabra Annals*, p 72
160. *Cabra Annals*, p 73

O'Reilly, Butler – but for the most part there were not many of their old Anglo-Irish families represented. A new era had come. Masters and Governesses were employed and Writing, Accounts, Arithmetic, Geography and use of the Globes were regular subjects. A Dancing Master was also engaged. Some of the text books and their prices have been recorded and the fees paid for tuition and 'offerings'. The offerings may have been for charity or a church offering.

	£	s	d
Goldsmith' English (abridged)	00	03	09
French Grammar	00	04	04
Thompson's Geography	00	06	00
Usher's Grammar	00	03	03
Fontaine's Fables	00	06	06
Chonbaud's Fables	00	02	02
Dancing Master	01	14	01
Easter Offering	00	05	00
Christmas Ditto	00	05	00
	04	12	10

The nuns were intent on keeping up standards for the girls in the school; the prospectus required that each young lady have a summer, winter and dancing costume. The Bellew organ had been brought from Channel Row and the nuns hired an 'organ boy' regularly to keep the bellows blowing in an effort to maintain the tradition of good church music for as long as possible. The nuns themselves made great efforts to restore the religious life and observances they had known in Channel Row and from this time forward they used their religious names with the prefix Sister. Thus Eliza Byrne became Sr Joseph, Lydia Wall, Sr Osanna, and Brigid Strong, Sr Catherine; they also wore the Dominican habit of white serge, a fact reflected in the laundry expenses.

The move from Channel Row to new surroundings seems to have given the nuns some new energy but the school never prospered as the Channel Row school had. Clontarf in those days was not regarded as a very healthy environment. The city dump was sited not far away on the site of the presentday

Fairview Park and the nuns' health suffered. Their financial situation did not improve very much and they still struggled with bad debts to the amount of £3440-15-6 when they settled in Clontarf. Another financial burden on them at that time were the taxes which had been increased after the 1798 rebellion:

Window tax	£07.07.06
Watch tax	£06.00.00
Jury Cess	£02.11.06
Minister's Money	£03.00.00
Paving & Lighting	£11.08.06

One very encouraging sign and the one which proved to be their salvation, was the arrival of four new members to the community; these young nuns made an enormous difference to the community. Sr Anne Columba Maher and Sr Magdalene Butler in particular were to become famous in community life in later years. Anne Columba developed the Cabra community and schools and Magdalene founded the Mount Street community which later moved to Sion Hill, Blackrock, Co Dublin. Another newly-gained friend of the community in the Clontarf phase, Fr Edmund Cruise OP was to be instrumental in persuading the nuns to move again, to leave Clontarf and re-locate in Cabra.

St Mary's Dominican Convent, Cabra
Eliza Byrne had entered the community in Channel Row when the nuns were at a very low point in their morale. They were ageing, the finances were scanty, lawsuits went against them, the school had closed and under Providence it is difficult to see how they could have survived as a group of Dominican women were it not for Eliza and her brother. Unfortunately we do not know his baptismal name. He came to their aid with advice, money and practical help in any way he could. Thanks to that help and Eliza's approach to their problems, the community was able to leave Channel Row and settle in Clontarf. The Dominican Provincial, Fr M. Coghlan, appointed Columba Maher as prioress in 1814 shortly after her profession. Columba became a friend of Fr Cruise OP of the Esker community in Galway; she met Edward Cruise in Clontarf and relied on his

advice about the future of the convent. The school in Clontarf closed after a relatively short time, eleven years, due to the small numbers and the lack of money to pay extern teachers. Fr Cruise was allowed by his superiors in Esker to help the nuns in every possible way and he looked for a property for a new foundation in Cabra on the north-west side of Dublin. In May 1819, the house in Cabra and seven acres of land was purchased.

The new house was taken in May 1819 but the nuns did not move from Clontarf until December following because there was still a half-year's lease on the Clontarf house. Three members did move as an emergency arose; Sr Osanna Wall was an invalid in rapidly declining health and it was thought that if she went to Cabra, the country air there would be more salubrious for her condition. Sr Osanna, Columba Maher and another nun left Clontarf in August but sadly the annals record 'the effort was too much for the patient and before dawn of the first morning following, she was released from her sufferings.[161]

Sr Osanna Wall and Sr Joseph/Eliza Byrne were the two who had gone through the closing years in Channel Row; to the former (Sr Osanna) in a general measure the community owed its preservation, for she brought with her a considerable dowry at a time when such temporal aid was sadly needed.[162]

On the 12 December 1819, the final transfer from Clontarf to St Mary's Dominican Convent Cabra, took place. The community at the time numbered five:

> Mother Mary (Anne) Columba Maher, Prioress
> Mother Mary Joseph (Eliza) Byrne, Sub-Prioress
> Sister Mary Teresa Dalton
> Sister Mary Dominic Dillon
> Sister Mary Magdalene Butler, novice[163]

Sr Joseph/Eliza Byrne was then the only living member of the Channel Row community to take up residence in the new convent in Cabra. She it was who provided the practical business-like approach in the transfer from Channel Row to Clontarf and had the will and the ability to bring the Dominicans further

---

161. *Cabra Annals*, p 82
162. Ibid
163. Ibid, p 83

along the road to survival. Sr Columba Maher, then a young prioress, was another capable leader. Her first concern when they settled in Cabra was to open what was called in those days, a 'poor school' that is a primary school giving free education to the children. Cabra was to flourish under her leadership and its many branches spread not only in Ireland but further afield to South Africa, America and Australia. These five women were the new guardians of a great tradition which has an historical validity of more than three and a half centuries. It goes even further back to the thirteenth-century foundation of the Order by St Dominic. Those who went through the hall door of their new house in Cabra in December 1819, brought with them the flame of the Dominican torch, the *Lucerna Christi*, whose light had been guarded by the generations from the original community in Galway in 1644. The years of exile in Spain in 1652 did not quench the flame; Juliana Nolan and Mary Lynch carried it back to Galway in 1686 and from there it was passed on to Mary Bellew and her companions and successors in Channel Row, Clontarf and Cabra.

CHAPTER ELEVEN

Reflections and Conclusion

Bernadette Cunningham in her article 'The Poor Clare Order in Ireland', writes of finding 'tantalising references to convents of Franciscan nuns in Ireland in the pre-Reformation period but there is no clear evidence of any Poor Clare foundations'.[164] The Dominican women have the same experience; in their case the written records date only from 1644 and, while there is speculation about Dominican 'convents' prior to that date, nothing can be definitively claimed as proof that such existed. One is struck by some close parallels between the Poor Clares and the Dominican women in Ireland in the seventeenth and eighteenth centuries. Both are medieval Orders which were introduced to Ireland by the friars of their respective Orders soon after the arrival of the Normans. Dominican friars came to Dublin in 1224, just three years after the death of their founder St Dominic. The women members' history can be historically verified only from the seventeenth century.

Confirmation of the Poor Clares and the Dominicans as legitimate members of their Orders was made in each case by provincial chapters of the friars: the Franciscan chapter held in Limerick in 1629 and the Dominican chapter in Kilkenny in 1643. In both cases the nuns' family background was Anglo-Norman. Both Orders were relatively strong in Galway in the seventeenth century and both found it necessary for safety reasons to make a foundation in Dublin in the early eighteenth century. Both were encouraged to do so by the same clerics in the Dublin archdiocese, Archbishop Edward Byrne and the Reverend Cornelius Nary. The Poor Clares previously had a convent in Dublin in 1620s but it did not survive.

164. B. Cunningham, 'The Poor Clare Order in Ireland' in *The Irish Franciscans 1534-1990* edited by E. Breathnach, J. MacMahon OFM and John McCaffrey (Dublin: Four Courts Press, 2009) pp 159-174

The Poor Clares who left Galway in 1712 are mentioned several times in our Channel Row story. They left Galway just five years before Mary Bellew and her companions went to Dublin in 1717. In the course of time the support of their relatives was crucial for their continuance though the nuns earned their living by opening on their own initiative, a kind of retirement home for ladies known as 'parlour boarders'. Both Orders also opened a girls' boarding school. The first Irish women to join the Poor Clares were those who left Ireland to join their convent in Gravelines in the Spanish Netherlands in 1607. Later in the century, in 1639, a Dominican convent was founded in Lisbon for young Irish women who wished to join the Order. Neither group of young women could have done this in Ireland at the time; Dominican nuns in Galway had to flee to Spain in 1652 due to harassment from the civil authorities.

Devotion to the church's liturgy was a strong feature of both Poor Clare and Dominican life and in their new surroundings in Dublin the solemn choral office and Mass were enhanced by good music. The Dominicans had an organ donated by the Bellew family, a well adorned chapel with a remarkable altarpiece 'after the manner of Van Dyck', while the Poor Clares opened' a very good chapel, with a handsome altar' and again an alterpiece depicting the crucifixion with panels depicting St. Francis and St. Clare.[165] The family names of Dillon, Nugent, Browne and others are common in both stories. When the Poor Clares came to Dublin in 1712 they lived in a convent in Channel Row which had been built for the Benedictines in the time of James II. In 1717, the Dominicans were given a lease of the same convent as their residence and lived there until 1808. The Poor Clares were forced to leave Channel Row shortly after their arrival due to the raid on the convent by the authorities. They then took up residence in North King Street. These close links in Irish history between the Poor Clares, who are daughters of St Francis of Assisi, and the daughters of St Dominic de Guzman, in the seventeenth and eighteenth centuries are reminders to present-day Poor Clares and Cabra Dominicans, of the close friendship which existed between St Francis of Assisi and St

---

165. B. Cunningham, 'The Poor Clare Order in Ireland', p 169

Dominic in the thirteenth century at the foundation of both Orders. As the old Irish proverb says: *'ar scáth a chéile, a mhaireas na daoine'* – we are all interdependent.

The seventeenth and eighteenth centuries was a time of unease and hardship for all Catholics in Ireland, for the laity no less than for the secular clergy and the men and women of the religious orders. Poverty was widespread; even before the Great Famine of 1847 occasional famine was experienced in the eighteenth century when crops failed. There was also real and immediate danger for them when rumours spread of a Stuart revival. The Dominican nuns both in Galway and Dublin must have spent many sleepless nights, fearful for their own safety and particularly when their Dominican brothers were in prison or perhaps 'on the run'. They would have known that in the living memory of their parents and grandparents, the executions took place of the Dominicans Terence Albert O'Brien and Peter Higgins of the Naas priory. Others also suffered the same fate. The nuns doubtless knew too the story of the two Honorias, Burke and Magean, from Mayo and of their deaths in Cromwellian times. They knew very well that this could still be their own fate, right up to the time and even after they left Galway.

All was not gloom and doom for them and as time passed and life became more normal they had their glory days when the school was flourishing and the parlour boarder ladies must sometimes have enlivened the day-to-day routine. The nuns even bought lottery tickets at times – the money spent on them is recorded in the *Account Books*. The eighteenth-century lotto was, as in our own time, a national lottery but there is nothing recorded in the *Account Books* about winnings. They must have had periods of quiet and stability when they were able to live normally and attend to the school and their religious duties in peace. One would hope that maybe they were able to have some pleasant experiences; perhaps hearing some of Handel's *Messiah* through the good offices of the musicians who attended their chapel on Sundays. If the *Adeste Fideles* was really sung in their chapel for the first time, was the occasion enhanced by the 'Italian musicians helping to make the voices of the Holy Sisters more melodious' as was claimed by the vicar of Naas, Stephen Radcliffe in 1725? However that may be, the Channel Row community could not have known that the *Adeste Fideles* would be a world-renowned carol in the centuries to come.

What were the thoughts of Mary Bellew and her companions as they left Galway in 1717 and again, how did Eliza Byrne and her three companions feel as the carriage drove away from Channel Row taking them to Clontarf in 1808? This was a departure which was to be repeated for Eliza as the carriage again took herself and Anne Columba Maher and the other three nuns to Cabra in 1819. We do not know how they managed to cope with these difficulties. They had no choice but to be practical and face up to their situation. Such was the faith that inspired them that they moved on with whatever courage they could muster. Whatever their experience of daily life, they certainly had great staying power and a determination to bring the Dominican way of life into the nineteenth century, and they succeeded. In the person of Anne Columba Maher, Providence had provided them with another woman of courage and foresight, who built up a flourishing community life in Cabra from the remnants of their own broken lives and that of their predecessors in Galway, Channel Row and Clontarf. That is our heritage.

As Sr Rose O'Neill's book names it, it is indeed *A Rich Inheritance*.

APPENDIX I

Statement to the Dublin Intelligence
15 September 1712
By the Lords, Justices and General Governors of Ireland

Whereon upon information given to Us the Lords Justices, that an Unlawful Society of Popish felons calling themselves Nuns was lately Translated from the Town of *Galway* to the City of *Dublin*, to be there Settled and Established by the Pretended Order of a Person calling himself Brother *John Burke* of the Order of St *Francis* and Provincial of *Ireland*, Testified under his Hand and Seal, We the Lords Justices gave immediate Directions for the Apprehension of the said Pretended Nuns and of the said *John Burke* and divers of the said Nuns have been since taken in the Habits of their Pretended Order but the said *John Burke* hath absconded himself and Fled from Justice: And whereas upon perusal of divers Papers it appeared to this Board that there are divers Popish Regulars in several parts of this Kingdom and that Doctor *Byrne* and Dr *Nary* of the City of *Dublin*, Popish Priests have presumed to Exercise Ecclesiastical Jurisdiction contrary to the Laws of this Kingdom or have respectively Aided and Assisted in the Exercise thereof, whereupon we the Lords Justices and Council give Directions for Apprehending them in order to their being Examined and further proceeded against according to Law; but the said Popish Felons have withdrawn themselves from their usual Places of Abode, that they cannot be Apprehended. To the End therefore that the food Laws made against Popish Archbishops and Bishops and Persons Using and Exercising Ecclesiastical Jurisdiction and Popish Regulars, may be put in due Execution and to prevent the above-named Persons from escaping the Hands of Justice, We the Lords Justices and Council, do think fit by this Our Proclamation, firstly to Charge and Command the Lord Mayor of the City of Dublin and all Justices of the Peace, Mayors, Sovereigns and other Magistrates, Sheriffs, Bailiffs, High and Petty Constables and all Her Majesty's Officers and Ministers of Justice within the limits of their respective Jurisdictions and Powers to Use their utmost Endeavours to Take and Apprehend the said *John Burke*, Dr *Byrne* and Dr *Nary* and to commit them and every of them to safe Custody and to give speedy Notice thereof to the Clerk of the Council, in order to their being prosecuted according to Law.

And We do hereby Will and Require all Her Majesty's Officers Civil and Military, and all other Her Loving Subjects to be Aiding and Assisting to the said Lord Mayor, Justices of the Peace, Magistrates and Officers in the Apprehending and Securing of the said Persons.

APPENDIX II

Excerpt from the Bellew and Browne Family Papers, by courtesy of Lord John Kilmaine *

E01 - CAPTAIN SIR JOHN BROWNE OF THE NEALE, 3rd BARONNET

Sir John [Browne] is the eldest son of Sir George, 2nd baronet. He married in May 1680, Anne, eldest daughter of George Hamilton, 3rd baron of Strabane, and of Elizabeth, daughter of Christopher Fagan, of Feltrim, in the county of Dublin.
Anne died, three months after her marriage on 14 August 1680.

John Browne re-married Julia (or Juliana) third daughter of Sir Patrick Bellew, 1st baronet, of Barmeath, or Bellew Mount, in the county Louth, and of Castle Bellew, in the county of Galway; and of Elizabeth, daughter of Sir Richard Barnwall, 2nd baronet de Crickstown.

Sir Patrick Bellew, High Sheriff of the County Louth (1687) having been created Baronnet of Ireland 11 December 1688. He was the son of Sir John Bellew of Lisrany and of Willystown, member of parliament for County Louth; and of Mary, daughter of Robert Dillon of Clonbrock.

The second son of Sir John, Christopher, of Corgarrowes, is the ancestor of the Bellews of Mount Bellew, in the county of Galway.

The Bellew family are the descendants of Sir Adam de Bella Aqua (Bellew) (13th century).

Captain John Browne was taken prisoner at the Siege of Derry (18 April -28 July 1689) on 6 May 1689 and abandoned James II after the defeat of the Irish at Aughrim, 12 July 1691.

He succeeded his father in May 1698

He had eleven children, three sons and eight daughters:

01 George, 4th baronet
02 John, 5th baronet
03 Henry, ancestor of the Brownes of Knockmore
04 Alice, who married George Aylmer, and later Dominick Meade
05 Elizabeth, who married George Browne, of Brownestown
06 Mary, who married Roger Palmer
07 Bridget, who married Richard McCormic
08 Julia, who became a religious [died in Channel Row Convent, March 1747] *
09 Henrietta, who married Thomas Fitzgerald of Turlough Park. She died in 1774
10 Mabel, who married Dominick Browne of Breaghwy

11 Anne, who married Kedagh Geoghegan
Sir John Browne died 11 April 1711. His will, dated 11 September 1700,
was ratified in 1712. The will of Lady Browne dated November 1728
was ratified on 10 May 1729.

* Document translated from French and section in brackets added

APPENDIX III

From *Account Book*, No 6
Channel Row Convent

January 1769

Expenses:

Butter man	£12.09s.05d
A bed for Miss Falvey	£02.10s.00d
Coach hire for Mrs Bourke to buy bed	£00.02s.02d
Miss Dace for bread	£00.02s.00d
Wages Rose Martin	£04.05s.04d
Earnest to the cooke	£00.01s.01d
Paid the cook to buy her shoes	£00.03s.03d
Mr Brullen for fixing bed	£00.02s.02d
Nails, bread	£00.00s.04d
Quire Directory	£00.00s.06d
Half dozen brooms	£00.00s.09d
2 mops	£00.01s.04d
Altar bread	£00.00s.06d
Turnips	£00.01s.09d
Potatoes	£00.03s.04d
Greens	£00.02s.02d
Mustard	£00.02s.04d
Fish	£00.11s.02d
Eggs	£00.05s.04d
A stone of male (meal)	£00.01s.02d
Spice and vinegar	£00.00s.03d
Oyle for jack	£00.00s.01d
A xmas box to Mrs Chaells man that brought ye wax lights	£00.02s.02d
For fouls for the lodgers at several times	£00.07s.10d
For tripes for the family	£00.01s.06d
A gallon of oyle for the Hall	£00.02s.08d
For a pot, a basin and plate for Miss Falvey	£00.01s.06d
For sellery, soap and candles	£00.07s.00d

Contracts:

Butcher	£00.16s.00d
Baker	£03.12s.04d
Butter, new	£02.11s.09d
Salt butter	£01.01s.03d
Fish	£01.02s.11d
Fowl	£02.07s.09d
Milk	£01.04s.02d
Sundries	£02.13s.00d

APPENDIX IV

LIST OF CHANNEL ROW NUNS 1717-1820

NOTE: (a) Abbreviations, k.n. not known
(b) All those named from Catherine Cruise onwards
were professed in Channel Row except the last three
nuns listed who were professed in Clontarf and Matilda
Butler who was professed in Cabra.
(c) Age at death given where known

NAME	PROFESSED	YEAR OF DEATH
Mary Bellew	1702, Galway	1726
Julia Browne	1712 "	1747
Elizabeth Weever	1712 "	1755
Honoria Vaughan	1713 "	1753
Alicia Rice	1714 "	1763
Ellen Keating	1713 "	1742
Mary Plunkett	n.k. "	1719
Catherine Cruise	n.k. "	1776
Rose O'Farrell	1719, Channel Row	1763 [aged 72 yrs]
Catherine Daly	1719	n.k.
Mary Kelly 1	n.k.	1749
Mary Kelly 11	n.k.	1780
Anastasia Wyse	c.1719	n.k.
Barbara Esmond	c.1720	1757 [aged 53 yrs]
Margaret Reily	c.1720	n.k.
Maria Daly	c.1720	n.k.
Mary Daly	n.k.	1757 [aged 52 yrs]
Sarah/Sally Dillon	c.1725	1776 [aged 75 yrs]
Mary/Maria Reily	c.1720	1757 [aged 53 yrs]
Elizabeth de Burgo	c.1722	1776 [aged 68 yrs]
Mary Welsh/Walsh	1724/25	1756
Catherine Reily	n.k.	1775 [aged 69 yrs]
Eleanor/Ellen Keating	1722	1782 [aged 81 yrs]
Mary Allen/Alen	1723	
Catherine Catto/Kelly	1725	1772 [aged 81 yrs]
Mary Donelan	1735	n.k.
Jane Bodkin	n.k.	1775 [aged 61 yrs]
Alicia/Ellis O'Kelly	c.1733	1754 [died young]

NAME	PROFESSED	YEAR OF DEATH
Jane Purcell	c.1737	1770 [aged 62 yrs]
Mary Nugent	1739	n.k.
Mary French 1	1744	1776
Elizabeth/Eliza O'Kelly	c.1748	1778 [aged 53 yrs]
Mary MacEgan	c.1748	1792 [aged 62 yrs]
Mary Kirwan	c.1750	1777 [aged 47 yrs]
Mary/Molly Kelly	1750	1786 [aged 60 yrs]
Susanna Berford	c.1752	n.k.
Anne/Nancy Blake	1755	1797 [aged 75yrs]
Eleanor Fottrell	1725	n.k.
Margaret/Peggy Horish	c.1726	1768 [aged 67yrs]
Dorothy Dease	c.1750	c.1777
Mary Maguire	c.1727	1791
Mabel/Bell Kirwan	1750	n.k.
Mary French 11	n.k.	1804
— Dowdall	n.k.	1788
Jane Reily	n.k.	1742
Eliza Byrne	c.1790 *	1742
Brigid C. Strong	1790s *	1830 in Cabra
Lydia O. Wall	1790s *	1814 in Clontarf
Bridget Bodkin	n.k.	1819 in Cabra
Anne Columba Maher	1809 Clontarf	1855 in Cabra
Maria Teresa Dalton	1818 Clontarf	1855 [aged 78 yrs]
Catherine D. Dillon	1819 Clontarf	1835 [aged 39 yrs]
Matilda M. Butler	1819 Cabra (first prof.) * Last nuns in Clontarf.	1856 [aged 57 yrs.] Died in Siena Convent.

Bibliography

PRIMARY SOURCES

MANUSCRIPT SOURCES
Annals of Cabra (typescript of first draft) n.d.
Account Books, Channel Row Books 1-8, 1719-1829
Papers of the Browne Family, the Neale, Co Mayo
Report of Dominican Provincial of Ireland to Master General 1767,
    Cabra Archives
The Correspondence of Teresa Mulally and Bessie Bellew 1786,
Archives of Presentation Convent, George's Hill, Dublin.

Printed Primary Sources
Kavanagh, Imelda OP, *Annals 1647-1912,* Dominican Convent, Cabra
Sleator, ed, *The Journals of the House of Lords* (Irish) Vols. 1-1V 1634-1776
    (Dublin: 1779-1782)

ALMANACKS, DIRECTORIES, NEWSPAPERS AND PAMPHLETS
Dublin Daily Post
Dublin Directory 1753
Dublin Intelligence
Complete Catholic Registry, Directory and Almanack 1836
Gentlemen's and Citizens' Almanack 1729
Hibernian Journal
Pue's Occurences
Radcliffe, S., *A Letter to the Reverend Edward Synge* (Dublin: 1725)
— *A Serious and Humble Enquiry* (Dublin: 1727)
Watson's Almanack 1741

BOOKS
De Burgo, T., *Hibernia Dominicana* (Cologne: 1762)
Fenning, H., ed, *The Fottrell Papers, 1721-39*; an edition of the papers
    found on the Person of Fr John Fottrell, Provincial of the
    Dominicans in Ireland, at his Arrest in 1739 (Belfast: Public Records
    Office Northern Ireland, 1980)
Harris, W., *The History and Antiquities of the City of Dublin* (Dublin: 1766,
    reprinted Ballynahinch, 1994)
O'Heyne, J., *The Irish Dominicans of the Seventeenth Century* (Louvain:
    1706). Reprinted with English translation by Fr A. Coleman
    (Dundalk: 1902)

Rogers, D. M., ed, Rodriguez A., *A Treatise of Modesty and Silence 1632* (English Recusant Literature, Vol 139) 1973
— Rodriguez A., *A Treatise of Humility 1632* (English Recusant Literature Vol 347)
— Rodriguez A., *A Treatise of Mental Prayer, 1627* (Scholar Press edition Vol 291) 1977

SECONDARY SOURCES

BOOKS, JOURNALS AND PERIODICALS
Aumann, J. *Spiritual Theology* (London: 1980)
— *Christian Spirituality in the Catholic Tradition* (London: 1985)
Bailey, J., ed, *The Diary of Lady Frederick Cavandish*, 2 Vols (London: 1927)
Ball, F. E., *A History of Co Dublin*, 6 Vols (Dublin: 1902-1920)
Beckett, J. C., *The Making of Modern Ireland, 1603-1923* (Dublin: 1966)
Boydell, B., *A Dublin Musical Calendar 1700-69* (Dublin, Irish Academic Press, 1988)
Brady, C. and Gillespie, R., *Natives and Newcomers, Essays on the Making of Irish Colonial Society, 1534-1641* (Dublin: 1986)
Brady, J., *Catholics and Catholicism in Eighteenth Century Press* (Maynooth: 1965)
Burke Savage, R., *A Valiant Dublin Woman* (Dublin: 1940)
De Caussade, J. P., *Self-Abandonment to Divine Providence* (Dublin: 1971)
— *The Sacrament of the Present Moment*, trs K. Muggeridge (London: 1981)
Chenevix Trench, C., *Grace's Card, Irish Catholic Landlords 1690-1800* (Dublin: 1997)
Clarke, A., *The Old English in Ireland 1625-1642* (London: 1966)
Concannon, H., *The Poor Clares in Dublin* (Dublin: 1929)
— *Irish Nuns in Penal Days* (Dublin: 1931)
Corish, P. *The Catholic Community in the Seventeenth and Eighteenth Centuries* (Dublin: 1981)
Cosgrove, J., 'Hiberniores Ipsis Hibernis', in *Studies in History Presented to R. Dudley Edwards*, Cosgrove and McCartney, eds (Dublin: 1979)
Craig, M., *The Architecture of Ireland* (London: 1982)
— *Dublin 1660-1860* (Dublin: 2006 edition)
Cullen, L. M., *Life in Ireland* (London: 1968)
— *An Economic History of Ireland since 1660* (London: 1972)
— *The Emergence of Modern Ireland 1600-1900* (London: 1981)
Curtis, E., *A History of Ireland* (London: 1937 3rd edition)
D'Alton, J., *The Memoirs of the Archbishops of Dublin* (Dublin 1838)
Day, A., ed, *Letters from Georgian Ireland* (Belfast: 1991)
Dickson, D., ed, *The Gorgeous Mask, Dublin 1700-1850* (Dublin: 1987)
Dominican Sisters, *Weavings; Celebrating Dominican Women* (Dublin: 1988)

Donnelly, N., *Short Histories of Dublin Parishes*, part X (Dublin: n.d.)
— *Roman Catholics, State and Condition of R.C. Chapels in Dublin 1749* (Dublin: 1904)
Fagan, P., *The Second City: Portrait of Dublin 1700-1760* (Dublin:1986)
— *Dublin's Turbulent Priest, Cornelius Nary 1658-1738* (Dublin: 1991)
Fenning, H., *The Undoing of the Friars of Ireland* (Louvain: 1972)
— *The Irish Dominican Province 1698-1797* (Dublin: 1990)
Finglas Environmental Heritage Project, *Finglas Through the Ages* (Dublin: 1994)
Gillespie, R. *The Sacred in the Secular: Religious Change in Catholic Ireland* (Vermont: 1993)
— *Devoted People: Belief and Religion in Early Modern Ireland* (Manchester: 1997)
Harvey, Karen J., *The Bellews of Mountbellew* (Dublin: 1998)
Henry, B., *Dublin Hanged* (Dublin: 1994)
Irish Ecclesiastical Record, February, May, September 1891 (Maynooth: 1891)
James, F. G., *Ireland in the Empire* (Cambridge, Mass, 1973)
Johnstone, E. M., *Great Britain and Ireland 1760-1800* (Edinburgh 1963)
— *Ireland in the Eighteenth Century* (Dublin, 1974)
Kealy, M., *Dominican Education in Ireland 1820-1930* (Dublin: Irish Academic Press, 2007)
Kelly, J. & Keogh, D., eds, *History of the Catholic Diocese of Dublin* (Dublin: Four Courts Press, 2000)
Komochak, J. A., Collins, M., Lane, D. A., eds, *The New Dictionary of Theology* (Dublin: 1987)
Lennon, C., *The Lords of Dublin in the Age of Reformation* (Dublin: 1989)
Lyons, F. S. L., ed, *Bicentenary Essays, Bank of Ireland 1783-1983* (Dublin: 1983)
MacCurtain, M., *Tudor and Stuart Ireland* (Dublin: 1972)
MacDonnell, J., ed, *Ecclesiastical Art of the Penal Era; Maynooth Bicentenary* (Maynooth, 1995)
MacLysaght, E., *Irish Families* (Dublin: 1957)
— *Irish Families, their Names Arms, and Origins* (Dublin: 1985)
McCabe, H., *A Light Undimmed: The Convent of Bom Successo, Lisbon* (Dublin: Dominican Publications, (2007)
Maxwell, C., *Ireland Under the Georges* (London: 1936)
McCready, C. T., *Dublin Street Names, Dated and Explained* (Dublin: 1982)
McNamara, J. A. K., *Sisters in Arms: Catholic Nuns Through Two Millennia* (Harvard: 1996)
McRedmond, L., *To The Greater Glory: A History of the Irish Jesuits* (Dublin: 1991)
Milne, K., *Irish Charter Schools* (Dublin: 1997)
Moody, T.W., Vaughan, W.E., eds, *A New History of Ireland 1681-1800 Vol IV* (Oxford: 1986)

Mooney, G., 'Mrs Bellew's Family' in *Dublin Historical Record*, Vol XXII, October 1968 (Dublin: 1968)

Ní Mhurchadha, M., *Fingal, 1603-60: Contending Neighbours in North Dublin* (Dublin: Four Courts Press, 2005)

O'Donnell, E. E., *The Annals of Dublin* (Dublin: 1987)

O'Neill, R., *A Rich Inheritance: Galway Dominican Nuns 1644-1994* (Galway: 1994)

O'Neill, T. P., *The Tribes and other Galway Families* (Galway: 1984)

Ordnance Survey, *Dublin Street Directory* (Dublin 1995)

Ó Tuama, S. and Kinsella T., eds, *An Duanaire: Poems of the Dispossessed* (Mountrath: 1981)

Peckham Magray, M., *Women Religious and the Devotional Revolution* (New York: 1998)

Pochin Mould, D. C., *The Irish Dominicans* (Dublin: 1957)

Power, T. P. and Whelan, K., eds, *Endurance and Emergence* (Dublin: 1990)

Simms, J. G., *Jacobite Ireland 1685-91* (London: 1969)

Sweeney, C. L., *The Rivers of Dublin* (Dublin: 1991)

Tugwell, S., *The Way of the Preacher* (London, 1979)

— ed, *Dominic*, Vladimir, Koudelka (London: 1997)

Wall, M., *The Penal Laws 1691-1760* (Dundalk, 1961)

Widdess, J. H. D., *The Richmond, Whitworth and Hardwicke Hospitals Dublin: 1772-1972* (Dublin: 1972)

Index